"If someone you love is harmfully using drugs, have you been told th true. *The Beyond Addiction Workbook for Families and Friends* is a co friends to follow, offering an impressive array of evidence-based tools explained in everyday language. Its Invitation to Change approach is just that: an invitation to consider and try out various practical things you can do to make a difference. It blends science and kindness with a wealth of clinical experience in helping people change."

—**William R. Miller, PhD,** emeritus distinguished professor of psychology and psychiatry at The University of New Mexico, and author of *Motivational Interviewing* and *On Second Thought*

"It looks like the Center for Motivation and Change has done it again. They have updated and enhanced their information regarding the best ways to work with individuals who have problems with substance use. Covering several evidence-based treatments, they have beautifully created a way for all substance-use providers to learn and use state-of-the-art, down-to-earth information. This is a workbook that should be on your desk."

—**Robert J. Meyers, PhD,** emeritus associate professor of psychology at The University of New Mexico; director of Robert J. Meyers, PhD & Associates; and creator of Community Reinforcement and Family Training

"An essential, empathetic, evidence-based, and hopeful guide for loved ones of people with addiction who want to help but often either don't know how or have been poorly advised about what actually works."

—**Maia Szalavitz,** author of *Undoing Drugs,* contributing opinion writer for *The New York Times,* and author or coauthor of seven other books

"When my son was addicted, our family was in turmoil. I was desperate to help my child—to save him—but the advice I got was unhelpful and some was dangerous. If only *The Beyond Addiction Workbook for Family and Friends* was available then. It's a godsend that can guide us from hell to healing."

—**David Sheff,** author of *Beautiful Boy*

"Sorely neglected in the world of addiction treatment are families and other loved ones of people who struggle with misuse of substances. For the first time, in *The Beyond Addition Workbook for Family and Friends,* three solid, science-based approaches shown to have greater benefit than those traditionally used in addiction treatment are woven together to bring about lasting change. From strategies to improve communication to ways to invite loved ones to enter treatment to using positive reinforcement in order to get the behavior you want, this workbook is loaded with practical, self-paced guide sheets and wisdom that will help families, friends, treatment professionals, and educators."

—**Anne M. Fletcher, MS,** author of *Inside Rehab, Sober for Good,* the *Thin for Life* books, and *Weight Loss Confidential*

"From the opening paragraph it's clear these authors know what they are talking about! They bring a fresh, scientific, and underused perspective to the crucial subject of helping a loved one address addictive problems. They balance a focus on taking care of yourself, and engaging in new and targeted efforts to help your loved one. This workbook sets a new standard for how to educate families about these issues."

—**Tom Horvath, PhD,** cofounder and past president of SMART Recovery; president of Practical Recovery Psychology Group; and author of *Sex, Drugs, Gambling, and Chocolate*

"When a loved one struggles with addiction, have you ever wondered how to keep your heart open, stay connected, be maximally helpful, and not become a martyr or an enabler? This remarkable program shows you how. Based on the solid science of mindfulness, acceptance, and compassion, this book will ease you into an entirely new mindset. Get ready to sigh with relief. Then just practice and see what happens."

—**Christopher Germer, PhD,** instructor of psychiatry at Harvard Medical School, codeveloper of the Mindful Self-Compassion Program, and coauthor of *The Mindful Self-Compassion Workbook*

"*The Beyond Addiction Workbook for Family and Friends* provides excellent guidance for people who deeply care for someone problematically using substances. As a psychologist, I've consulted with world-class clinics whose main aim is helping people with substance concerns, and I wish I had this workbook as a resource to train professionals and laypersons about these effective techniques for change. The authors provide a great deal of practical, impactful support and direction for you."

—**D.J. Moran, PhD, BCBA-D,** founder of Pickslyde Consulting, and coauthor of *ACT in Practice*

"One of the most overlooked aspects of the experience of those who are tangential to recovery—those that have a partner or child or friend or family member that struggle with addiction—is how much of a growth opportunity it can be for them personally; and in fact is a requirement for any kind of transformation to take place. There is a dearth of dynamic and effective resources available for this population; this workbook is the gold standard. If you want to put compassionate, effective, transformational, and evidence-based practices into use to help both yourself and your loved one, you absolutely need this workbook."

—**Holly Whitaker,** author of *Quit Like a Woman*

The Beyond Addiction Workbook for Family & Friends

EVIDENCE-BASED SKILLS TO
HELP A LOVED ONE MAKE POSITIVE CHANGE

Jeffrey Foote, PhD | Kenneth Carpenter, PhD
Carrie Wilkens, PhD

New Harbinger Publications, Inc.

Publisher's Note

This publication is designed to provide accurate and authoritative information in regard to the subject matter covered. It is sold with the understanding that the publisher is not engaged in rendering psychological, financial, legal, or other professional services. If expert assistance or counseling is needed, the services of a competent professional should be sought.

NEW HARBINGER PUBLICATIONS is a registered trademark of New Harbinger Publications, Inc.

New Harbinger Publications is an employee-owned company.

Distributed in Canada by Raincoast Books

Copyright © 2022 by Jeff Foote, Carrie Wilkens, and Kenneth Carpenter
New Harbinger Publications, Inc.
5720 Shattuck Avenue
Oakland, CA 94609
www.newharbinger.com

Cover design by Amy Daniel

Acquired by Jess O'Brien

Edited by Joyce Wu

All Rights Reserved

Library of Congress Cataloging-in-Publication Data on file

Printed in the United States of America

26 25 24

10 9 8 7 6 5 4 3

Contents

INTRODUCTION

An Invitation to You

Welcome!

If you picked up this guide because you love or care about someone using substances in a problematic way, there's a good chance you're dealing with a lot. You may be experiencing disappointment that your family is not "normal" or that the dreams you had for this person may never be realized; anger at the situation, at them, or at yourself for not being able to solve their problems; fear that they'll hurt themselves or you or maybe even die; shame at the thought that you somehow failed them or even that you may in some way be the cause; or isolation because you can't talk to others about what you and your loved one are going through. All these feelings and reactions are completely normal, valid, and hard to bear. One parent described it like this:

> *We have been through some stuff as a family, but nothing could have prepared us for our daughter falling down the well of drug use. It's been two years of long nights, a knot in my stomach, and tears and fights between all of us, including my husband and me. Thank God we have a road map now, because we were driving in the dark for a long time, and there is no worse feeling.*

Helping someone struggling with substance use can be a very lonely journey, made worse by lack of understanding, fear, and the impact of stigma and shame. You want to help this person make positive changes in their life, but you've probably heard people say things like "Once an addict, always an addict" or "They won't change until they hit rock bottom," making you feel as if there's nothing you can do to help. You may have been told you're "codependent" or "an enabler," which in turn has led you to believe that you shouldn't help or that you have a problem yourself. And to top it all off, the pejorative words commonly used to describe the person you care about ("alcoholic," "addict," "dirty," "junkie") are loaded with stigma, shame, and pessimism about the potential for change.

If any of this sounds familiar, we're glad you found this guide.

If you thought your only options were demanding change with fights, ultimatums, and interventions or, conversely, that there's nothing you can do, you may be relieved to know there's a kinder and more effective way that you can help someone. This guide will show you how. Welcome to a new approach to helping: the Invitation to Change.

The Invitation to Change Approach

The Invitation to Change (ITC) will help you see your loved one's behavior in a whole new way: as something that serves a purpose for them and in some way makes sense. This approach gives you reasons that you can both understand and work with to motivate your loved one to change and to help them sustain that change. ITC will show you tools and strategies that invite and encourage change in your loved one, in yourself, in your family, and if you're inspired to share it, in your larger community. Here is what this guide can help you learn to do:

- Lessen the tension, conflict, and heated emotion in your relationship and household through new understanding and a fresh perspective on the situation.

- Give yourself permission and encouragement to make room for you, to allow yourself to be part of the change process and taken care of on this journey.

- Talk to your loved one in ways that are more likely to be heard—and listen in ways that are more likely to get them talking. In other words, improve collaboration. This includes a proven strategy for talking to them about their getting professional help (chapter 8).

- Respond more effectively both to the positive changes your loved one makes and to their less positive behaviors, while letting natural consequences play a role in motivating change (in a way that can be hard to do with traditional approaches to substance problems).

You may have picked up this book with mixed feelings that include hopefulness and curiosity (otherwise, why bother reading?) as well as skepticism and caution, as you've likely been hurt, confused, disappointed, and angered by your experiences so far. There is room for all these feelings in the Invitation to Change.

> ITC strategies will help you create the conditions for change, which in turn will make space for your loved one to consider positive change, start to change, and sustain that change over time.

The information, strategies, and techniques in ITC come from the experiences of researchers and clinicians who have spent years working with people in a variety of communities who struggle with substance use, as well as with their families. One thing we know from fifty years of research is that family involvement in helping someone who's struggling with substances is one of the most powerful predictors of entering treatment (Miller, Meyers, and Tonigan 1999; Meyers et al. 1999) and an important part of positive outcomes (Ariss and Fairbairn 2020). It's also one of the least utilized ways of helping people in the current treatment system (Grant et al. 2015).

You may be a relative, friend, coach, counselor, clergy member, or other non-relative of the person you'd like to help. For simplicity's sake, we use the terms *family* and *loved one* even though this guide is appropriate for anyone who wants to support positive change for someone using substances. When you see these words, feel free to substitute the type of relationship you have with the person you're hoping to help.

As you explore the ideas and exercises in this guide, keep in mind that you're part of a community of people who have tried these different approaches and maybe not gotten them exactly right the first time (or the second or the third), but were willing to continue learning, practicing, caring, and supporting each other. Please consider this our invitation to you: let yourself begin to be less isolated, stay connected to your loved one when you can, be a bit more compassionate toward yourself, and use this book to guide you to make a positive difference in your loved one's life.

Welcome to this community of science, kindness, and change. You *can* create an environment where change is more likely to happen by learning a new perspective on your loved one's behavior, including yourself in the change process with self-compassion, and learning new ways to talk and act. You *can* transform your current situation into one that is more livable, satisfying, and in line with your values; one that encourages, motivates, and supports your loved one's making healthier choices. The potential for change is great.

You *Can* Help

To summarize what research, clinical work, and families have learned over the past five decades: there is reason to be hopeful. People do change, and you can help.

If you love someone with a substance use problem, you may have been told to "detach with love" or to practice "tough love." And if you haven't followed this advice, you may have been told that you're "codependent." You may be confused about your role and may even believe that being caring toward your loved one is somehow causing the problem. But the research evidence is clear: you can help a loved one struggling with substances by actively supporting them. In fact, family influence is an important reason for seeking treatment for substance problems (Marlowe et al. 2001). While you're likely worn down and may want to walk away at times, you have permission to keep caring. The key, as you'll see in chapter 9, is in being strategic about when, where, and how you show it. We hope that the Invitation to Change helps you bring compassion, patience, and encouragement to every step in this process of helping and that you'll adopt the same outlook toward yourself.

The most effective methods for helping someone with a substance problem go by several different names, but they boil down to two key ingredients: science and kindness. Science and kindness help people change. We developed the Invitation to Change to bring evidence-based principles and practices, including kindness, into everyday relationships.

It may sound too simple and a bit soft, but kindness is the glue that holds the ideas and practices in ITC together and makes them meaningful and sustainable. You may have noticed that when people are frustrated, hurt, angry, and at their wits' end in a relationship, often kindness is in short supply. As you learn more about ITC and start to bring it into your life, we hope you'll allow kindness to be part of the change you want to see.

And the science? ITC includes elements and strategies from several evidence-based treatments, a few of which we single out below:

- Community Reinforcement and Family Training (CRAFT), developed by Drs. Robert Meyers and Jane Ellen Smith, promotes specific family strategies that encourage and support positive changes, improve communication, and allow the natural consequences of substance use to play a role in motivating change (Meyers, Villanueva, and Smith 2005). CRAFT also emphasizes family members' taking better care of themselves. Compared to families trained to do interventions, or who attend Al-Anon or other 12-step-based family self-help, CRAFT-trained families are significantly more likely to see their loved one's willingness to get help increase (Miller, Meyers, and Tonigan 1999) and substance use decrease or stop altogether (Brigham et al. 2014). It has also been shown to help the whole family feel better at every stage along the way to change (and even in the minority of cases when the loved one doesn't change).

- We've also added powerful elements from an approach called motivational interviewing (MI), developed by psychologists William Miller and Stephen Rollnick, which aims "to strengthen personal motivation for and commitment to a specific goal by eliciting and exploring the person's own reasons for change within an atmosphere of acceptance and compassion" (Miller and Rollnick 2013, 29). As research has demonstrated, how we talk to people about change can significantly impact their motivation and behavior (Amrhein et al. 2003; Smedslund et al. 2011). With ITC, you'll learn a variety of ways to encourage your loved one's motivation and support positive change.
- We know that you're reading this because you care deeply for your loved one and your family and sincerely want your situation to change. We also know that while the things and people we care about the most are what make life sweet, they can cause the most fear, frustration, hurt, and pain. When what is most important to us also causes distress, we're faced with a choice: we can walk away to try to avoid the pain, or we can take a step *toward* the source of upsetting emotion. Truly, there are benefits and costs to both directions. Acceptance and commitment therapy (ACT) recognizes pain and discomfort as a sign that something is important, and not as a reason to push away from the experience (Hayes, Strosahl, and Wilson 2012). When we're guided by our deepest values, we can withstand the vulnerability and pain in the service of what we love and the kinds of people we want to be. ACT strategies have been extensively researched and proven to help people stay connected to what is important, even when it's uncomfortable to do so.

You'll find books and journal articles listed in the back of this guide in case you want to dig deeper into the literature, but to sum it up: There is reason to be hopeful. People do change, and you can help.

How to Use This Guide

Since ITC is about creating the conditions for change to take place, it does not offer specific answers about treatment programs or medications. Instead, ITC is a process; a process of developing your understanding, increasing your self-awareness, and applying strategies that work for substance use, as well as for many other communication and behavior challenges. The chapters of this book take you through The Wheel—a holistic picture of the components of the Invitation to Change—from how to reframe your understanding of the problem, to increasing your awareness of yourself in the change process, to practical communication and behavior tools that promote change.

First are ideas crucial to understanding the situation you and your loved one are in: namely, that behaviors make sense in their contexts, one size doesn't fit all, and ambivalence about change is normal. Second are awareness skills of self-awareness, willingness, and self-compassion. And third are the action strategies to adjust your behavior and communication in ways proven to help motivate your loved one to change. Finally, practice, essential to getting the hang of any new skill or idea, forms the hub of the wheel.

The images in each part of the wheel are meant to help you remember the concepts and how they relate to each other. You can refer to them when you're struggling, in moments when you might say to yourself, *Geez, I feel like yelling, what other options do I have?*

This whole guide is organized around this wheel. But first, let's introduce you to each part with an overview so that when you get to the rest of the chapters and exercises, you'll already know why they're worth the effort.

Helping with Understanding: A New Perspective Matters

Behaviors make sense. We all engage in a variety of behaviors (such as reading, exercising, going to religious services, going dancing, protesting, gardening, going back to school, getting a tattoo, taking pain pills, eating cookies, drinking wine) because they're valuable to us for some reason. They help us feel good, reduce depression and anxiety, or bring us closer to what we believe to be worthwhile in life; perhaps they help us feel connected to our friends, improve focus, or alleviate pain. The pull to use substances is similar to any other behavioral choice we make: if it works in some way, we keep doing it. If using substances were as straightforwardly unrewarding as touching a hot stove, your loved one would have stopped already—hence, the image in the wheel. Understanding a person's reasons for their behavior is a crucial part of helping them change, as you'll see. To be clear, understanding does not mean agreeing with or liking. It does mean doing your best to put your own strong feelings and judgments to one side as you determine how you want to respond.

Understanding how your loved one's behavior makes sense to *them* invites connection and collaboration between you.

One size does not fit all. Substance use makes sense in different ways for different people. Every individual using substances and their family are unique. Likewise, there are many paths to change; what works for one individual and one family may not be right for the next. The current scientific evidence indicates psychological, biological, and social factors are all in play in substance use and substance use disorders (Marlatt et al. 1988; Uhl, Koob, and Cable 2019), and the mix of factors for each person is different. We also know that substance use disorders fall on a continuum of severity (Hasin et al. 2013) and can be positively influenced at any time.

Understanding that one size does not fit all invites you and your loved one to find a way to change that works for them.

The evidence is clear: labels are not helpful (Yang et al. 2017). We invite you to put aside the question of whether someone is an "addict" or an "alcoholic," because it simply does not matter. Labeling a person can shut down the process of exploring why their behavior makes sense to them. A ready-made answer such as "You're an alcoholic" often ends the discussion and tells us nothing about how best to move forward. People confuse labels with understanding; in fact, labels get in the way of understanding. Ultimately, blanket assumptions of what "addicts" and their families all need are stigmatizing and harmful. The reality is, people can be helped, and their individual reasons for using substances need to be understood as part of a customized helping process.

Ambivalence is normal. Ambivalence about change is to be expected. Since your loved one's substance use makes sense to them in some way, when they start to add in new, more constructive behaviors while simultaneously giving up the old substance behaviors, they will naturally have times when they feel pulled from both directions. They will have moments when they think, *I'm not so sure about this*! Change often happens in small steps—some forward, some sideways, some backward, but rarely in a straight line. Feeling ambivalent at any point in a process of change does not mean someone is being stubborn or "in denial"—it means they're remembering, and perhaps turning back to, what has worked in the past. Change is an ongoing process, not an end result; this is true for your loved one and for you. Expect it to take time.

Understanding that ambivalence is normal invites your loved one to examine their behavior from all sides, to weigh the pros and cons of old and new behaviors, and to find a balance that works for them.

Helping with Awareness: Helping Yourself Helps You Help Someone Else

Self-awareness lets you be you (and choose who you really want to be). Self-awareness includes awareness of your thoughts, feelings, body sensations, and reactions. It also includes awareness of your values—what you care about most deeply. It's likely you have feelings and values of love, hope, connection, patience, and cooperation. It's also likely you're struggling with a lot of fear, pain, and upset. Helping means allowing both the values and the pain because ignoring pain and fear often backfires, steering our behavior in ways we don't intend.

When you're aware of you, it helps you help them. Starting here, painful as it may be, brings compassion into your invitation to change, which is an invitation more likely to be accepted.

Willingness is a new way to relate to pain. You can learn to be willing to accept difficult feelings without trying to control them or shut them down. It's normal to want to eliminate discomfort and return to "how things used to be." Unfortunately, wishing that things were different does not often work and can eat up valuable time, energy, and hope. Instead, you can learn to embrace the fact that your reality includes pain, and begin to understand its connection to your caring, optimism, and desire to help. It's next to impossible to invest emotionally without also experiencing pain. Conversely, shutting out the pain by shutting down, withdrawing, or getting angry can mean losing touch with what matters most to you.

Willingness is an invitation to yourself—"Are you willing to allow for the vulnerability and pain that come with caring?"

Self-compassion goes the distance. Acknowledging your pain and your values can bring you compassion for all you're going through, and this can be deeply meaningful and sustaining. Certainly, self-compassion will take you farther than self-blame or shame. Since helping someone can be a stressful and painful process, self-compassion also includes self-care. People in emergency-helper mode often forget to take time for themselves, get enough sleep, find small pleasures, keep in touch with friends, and so on, but your emotional resilience, physical health, social supports, and perspective on change are all important parts of the process of change. To paraphrase the classic airplane safety announcement: we need to secure our own oxygen masks before assisting others. Practicing self-awareness, self-kindness, and self-care will sustain your helping efforts, and—as an added benefit—model behaviors that you hope to see from your loved one.

Self-compassion brings kindness and care to you, to sustain you through an invitation to sustainable change in your loved one. Taking care of yourself also invites them to do the same.

Helping with Action: How We Talk and How We Act

Good communication turns red lights green. The words we use and the way we use them matter, a lot. When someone you love is using substances or engaging in other risky behaviors, it's normal to find yourself expressing your feelings by yelling, lecturing, or shutting down—maybe even swearing or throwing things. Unfortunately, this approach takes attention away from the problem at hand and puts it on you instead: "You drank too much last night!" is met with "You're always yelling and being so negative, I can't do anything right for you!" And telling them what they should do is met with "you're not the boss of me" pushback. (Consider how you reacted the last time someone told you what to do instead of asking you what you wanted to do.) The way we communicate can cause the person we're speaking with to push back against what we're saying or step forward with us.

Communication that is collaborative—instead of controlling, confrontational, one-sided, or dismissive of your loved one's perspective—decreases defensiveness and invites conversations that support change.

Your behavior shapes theirs. In addition to the words we use, how we act and react can increase a loved one's positive behaviors and decrease negative ones. Someone who's trying to give up substances will likely need to overhaul multiple areas of their life: how they think, work, manage their feelings, relate to their bodies, connect with family and friends, and view themselves. For most, confidence is low and the skills they need to make such changes are just developing. You can contribute to their motivation and confidence if you notice, acknowledge, and reward any progress they make, even if it doesn't relate to substances. Start with celebrating small victories; they can grow larger over time. And when negative behaviors occur (and they will, since your loved one, like you, is only human), allowing their natural, negative consequences to occur will help decrease those behaviors over time, as will setting reasonable limits.

To be clear, negative behavior in the form of physical or emotional abuse is not okay. If you or other family members don't feel safe, please see the list of emergency resources at the end of this book. See also our discussion in chapter 9 about setting limits, which may help you sort out distress that you can tolerate from abuse that you can't. As long as the situation is safe for you, however, we encourage you to notice any positive steps your loved one takes toward change while you set boundaries you can live with.

Recognizing and rewarding positive change invites it to happen more, while allowing natural consequences to occur and setting respectful limits discourage negative behavior.

Practice, practice, practice. Practice is the hub (and sometimes the rub) of the ITC wheel, since nothing new can happen without learning and practice. Many of the ITC tools and strategies might go against what feels natural or is your habit. Our suggestions might also go against what you've been told to do by other professionals. We hope you find the willingness and patience to try doing things differently and then practice. And practice. And practice. You won't do it the way you wanted or planned every time, and that's okay; it's part of the process. Give yourself room to make mistakes and try to let the discouraging moments roll past. And as you notice how hard it is to change your own behaviors, we hope this awareness translates into a greater understanding of how hard it is for your loved one to change as well.

Now that we've explained the ITC Wheel, we'd like to suggest going through the chapters consecutively, as we've ordered the concepts and exercises in ITC to build on each other. But feel free to skip around—if you're drawn to an idea or topic in a different order, go ahead! If you're reading about positive reinforcement but have had three intense fights this week, you might shift to one of the strategies in the chapter on communication or to being aware of your reactions in the chapter on self-awareness. Ultimately, you can use this guide however works best for you. You might read it beginning to end in one sitting. You might work through it on your own, or with a group in your community. We encourage you to read the whole book over time because the parts fit together as a whole, but each chapter can also stand alone, if that is all you want to take in. The material is meant to be approachable, easy to understand, and available to you at different stages in the helping process. We say it about your loved one in chapter 2 and we cannot stress this enough for you, too: one size does not fit all; each person, family, community, and situation is different.

We also encourage you to use the exercises and worksheets to practice the skills in ITC as many times as you want or need. There are various worksheet versions of the exercises in this book available for download at the publisher's website: http://www.newharbinger.com/50188. (You'll also find a glossary of terms at the end of this book and on the website. See the very back of this book for details.) And, since we couldn't fit every worthy exercise in this book, you'll find even more exercises on our website at http://www.motivationandchange.com/family-services. As we continue to develop more resources for family and friends, we'll add them to our website. Some examples in the worksheets may not apply to your situation exactly, but we've done our best to capture a range of experiences. We also list resources you can consult to address more specific concerns at the end of this book.

Occasionally, we reference a book that two of us wrote with our colleague Nicole Kosanke, PhD, called *Beyond Addiction: How Science and Kindness Help People Change* (Foote, Wilkens, and Kosanke 2014). It would make a good (but not necessary) companion to this guide, should you find yourself wanting more of the theory behind an idea or more explanation of how or why something works. For example, in this guide we mention biological factors affecting substance use only in passing, but discuss them more comprehensively in *Beyond Addiction.* Plus, this guide offers you more exercises and plenty of blank space, but if you get tired of doing exercises and just want to curl up with a book that makes you feel understood, you might want to get *Beyond Addiction*, too.

Together with practice, these ways of understanding, being aware, and taking action add up to a powerful invitation to change. We'll continue to refer to The Wheel as we explore each part of it in more detail. We hope it helps you remember the science and kindness that help people change.

It takes effort to be a force for good, and we applaud you for finding the energy and courage to pick yourself up in the middle of these difficulties and learn new ways to help. Thank you, truly. Take care of yourself, communicate, learn the behavioral strategies, practice—and trust that things will change. This guide is full of useful information and ways to support you for the long haul. It is not a quick fix. We welcome you to this community of people trying to help a loved one. We hope this guide helps you in that effort and marks the beginning of positive, ongoing change.

Words from a fellow traveler: *Hi, my name is Lara, and my adult daughter suffers from mental disorders as well as substance abuse. Until I found ITC, I struggled greatly with the words "enabling," "rock bottom," and "codependence." Thanks to ITC, I learned that everything I've been taught about helping my daughter with addiction that made me feel awful does not have to be part of recovery. My daughter is still struggling, but things have improved vastly, and I no longer feel like crap about myself and how I am helping her. This has changed my life.*

PART ONE

Helping with Understanding

In this part, we offer new ways to see your loved one's behavior and your situation. By looking at the problem you face from a different perspective, you can start to create an environment in your home and a sense of possibility in your relationship that will help everyone take steps toward positive change.

A new understanding includes these key ideas:

- Your loved one has reasons and motivations for using substances that make sense and are important to them; otherwise, they would stop.
- Reasons for substance use differ for each person; they may evolve over time, but they're specific and important to that person.
- Change is a process of finding an alternative behavior and taking the time to develop it into a habit. That is, change is not simply a matter of quitting, but of shifting to do something different.
- New, alternative behaviors compete with the old ones, which were providing (and still could provide) some kind of value to your loved one.
- When we devalue something that someone values, such as substance use, we set them up to defend their behavior and choices even more.
- When we judge someone's behavior rather than understand it, they may not want to talk about it at all with us. They may hide their use, stop communicating, and not tell us the truth.
- When we understand someone's behavior, it invites them to talk about it and gives them room to consider downsides and alternatives.
- It will take time for new behavior(s) to make more sense and feel more comfortable than the old.

What Is the Impact of Understanding?

Understanding these ideas and acting with them in mind will have two big impacts—the first on you, the second on your loved one in turn.

- On you: Knowing why someone is doing something can affect how much you want to help. It increases empathy for your loved one and can incline you to step toward them rather than away. It can also help you be less reactive to their behavior.
- On your loved one: Feeling understood has a big impact on most of us! That, in combination with your increased empathy and lower reactivity, will set the stage for your loved one to be less defensive, more engaged, and ultimately in charge of their own change process.

The topics in this part of ITC build a foundation for the other parts of helping (through awareness and through action) that follow. We recommend that you read part 1—the first three chapters—before the others, since your understanding of the problem you face can be the difference between effectively helping your loved one or not.

Words from a fellow traveler: *I used to think my son was just being lazy and disrespectful when he used drugs. I was furious at him all the time and couldn't believe I had raised him so poorly. I now have a better understanding of why he does what he does and can talk to him about that. I still want him to stop but I can see why that is hard for him. We can have conversations about this and we don't end up fighting, which helps us both a lot.*

CHAPTER 1

Behaviors Make Sense

Understanding how your loved one's behavior makes sense to them invites connection and collaboration between you.

They're using because they're an addict. That's what addicts do.

Using drugs is crazy. Doesn't he see the consequences?

She's just self-destructive. She doesn't care what happens to her.

He'll manipulate to get what he wants. He has no moral compass.

These are only a few common reactions to substance use that you might have heard from others or had yourself. While such notions are understandable, they're based on misconceptions and confusion that are ubiquitous in our culture, and they're not helpful. They seem to be making sense of a person's behavior, but they're really just assumptions and judgments. They don't lead to true understanding.

But we can trace many of these unhelpful ideas circulating about substance use back to some important—and potentially very helpful—questions:

- Why would someone want to use drugs or alcohol in the first place?
- Why do they continue to use when it causes so much pain and destruction for us and for them?
- Why don't they just stop? It doesn't make sense. Maybe they haven't suffered enough to want to change?

In this chapter, we explore the why behind substance use, and offer evidence-based answers for why people use that might be new to you. If you can understand your loved one's behavior from their perspective, it invites connection and collaboration between you. Recognizing the function that substance use serves in their life decreases reactivity and increases compassion on your part, and decreases defensiveness and increases responsibility on theirs.

A New Perspective on Your Loved One's Behavior

Any behavior that we repeat serves a purpose—even behaviors that seem to have real downsides. People don't use substances because they're crazy. They don't use substances because they're bad. They use substances because they get something that they like, want, or need out of using them.

As living beings that have evolved to adapt, our actions are powerfully motivated by what happens next: if we behave a certain way and something good happens, we're more likely to repeat or increase that behavior. These good things can come from outside of ourselves, such as recognition from others (a raise, a pat on the back, a compliment) or from inside of ourselves (a feeling of calm, a positive mood, less anxiety). Conversely, we naturally decrease or stop a behavior if it doesn't work or if something negative happens, like when we touch a hot stove.

Many of the things that people get from using substances—often reliably and with an immediate effect—are understandable human wants or needs: to mellow out when we're anxious, to feel part of something, to feel less bored, to get to sleep—the list goes on. Though our individual priorities may differ, we can all understand wanting or needing these things. All such desired outcomes, however we achieve them, are **reinforcers** and make it likely that the behavior that causes them will be repeated. Behaviors that are reinforced are more likely to happen again, whether it be using a substance or getting a haircut. Meanwhile, behaviors that are *not* reinforced (because the outcome was either not good or nonexistent) are less likely to happen again, and over time, tend to stop.

Simply put, substance use is reinforced in one of two ways (or both): it adds something good to life, like human connection or pleasure, or it takes something uncomfortable away, such as anxiety, depression, boredom, physical pain, or withdrawal symptoms. A person's substance use does in fact make sense in some way that is reinforcing to them. And we need to understand that to help them change.

PAUSE BUTTON

1. We invite you to pause and ask yourself this question: What is it that my loved one gets out of substance use? Being curious about the "why" can help you make sense of their behavior and choices. It's also important to be aware that the why might be complicated depending on your loved one's life experiences, and your own. You can write your thoughts down here.

___

___

___

___

___

___

2. Do you notice any uncomfortable or upsetting feelings as you consider this question? Maybe you found yourself feeling frustrated, stuck, or heartbroken, or thinking things like "Why should I care what they get out of it?" Consider what you're feeling and write it down here.

___

___

___

___

It's normal to experience a variety of difficult emotions when you think about what might be reinforcing your loved one's behavior; you're still left with all that you don't like about it even if you understand it. We hope that over time you can learn to focus on the answer to the first question, even in the presence of anger or distress from the second, because it can lead to opportunities for further discussion, connection, and change.

Generally, the power of reinforcement for specific behaviors comes from three ingredients: the immediacy of whatever it is that reinforces the behavior, the consistency of the reinforcement, and how meaningful the outcome of the behavior is to the person practicing it.

- **Immediacy:** The quicker the outcome, or reinforcement, follows the behavior, the more powerful the learning experience and the stronger the behavior becomes. The effect of taking a drink or a "hit" is pretty immediate, making many substances powerful reinforcers.
- **Consistency:** The more consistently the reinforcement follows the behavior, the more powerful the learning experience. The short-term positive effects of using drugs or having a drink are remarkably predictable and consistent.
- **Meaningfulness:** The more valued the outcome, the stronger the learning experience. If feeling socially connected is important to your loved one and using drugs makes that easier to accomplish, then the behavior will be powerfully reinforced.

You might still be thinking, *They're using so much, it makes no sense at all at this point!* or *They might die from it, how on earth does that make sense?* We know it can be hard to be understanding when someone you care about is making choices that are maddening, scary, and potentially life threatening. Substance use affects the brain and body, so at a certain point your loved one may be using just to feel "normal" or to be able to get up and face the day. The physical dependency that people sometimes experience is also a powerful reason to continue substance use, when not using leads to withdrawal, feeling awful, and possibly medical complications. In any case, at any level of severity, understanding what is reinforcing about someone's behavior—why it makes sense to them—is key to getting them the help that they need.

Why Understanding That Behaviors Make Sense Matters

Looking at your loved one's behavior from this perspective—that behaviors meet certain needs, that they're reinforced in some way, and that behaviors and reinforcements make sense on some level, even if that sense isn't immediately apparent to you—helps in important ways:

- It shows you a different way forward. Knowing that someone's behaviors make sense to them lets you see what is happening before they choose to use substances, which can give you clues about what could happen instead. Is Friday night "blow off steam from my crappy job" night? Maybe you help them find another pressure relief valve. If you hear "Sleep is impossible without my weed," maybe you can help start a healthy sleep routine that you both follow and hold each other to. Understanding a person's choices can lead you to other, healthier ways for them to get those positive outcomes.

- It lowers your distress level. Understanding what someone gets from using can lower your fear and anxiety, as it makes the behavior seem less random and more predictable. If your loved one smokes to reduce social anxiety, you know they're more at risk when they're out socializing than at home with the family. Recognizing this won't eliminate your fear, but understanding the part of their choice that "makes sense" can significantly reduce the scary feeling of chaos and unpredictability. And as you learn the helping strategies later in this book, you'll be equipped to influence these patterns in positive directions.

- It helps you step toward them instead of away. Understanding the ways that someone's behavior makes sense to them will help you take it less personally and feel more empathy toward them. Feeling more connected to their motives and perspective can give you the energy you need to help your loved one make changes. Instead of thinking that they're irresponsible or torturing you, you can recognize the underlying loneliness, insecurity, depression, or boredom. The net effect is an increased desire to help on your part, instead of a desire to push them away.

- It increases collaboration on their end. A final benefit of understanding another person's behavior—instead of just being upset about it—is that it can help them feel understood, which will make them more likely to collaborate on a plan for change.

With these insights in mind, let's take a moment to consider the kinds of basic wants and needs that we can all relate to. We'll start with you.

Read the list below and check the boxes that apply to you.

Things I want/need in my life:

- ☐ To feel less or no anxiety
- ☐ To not feel depressed
- ☐ To feel good/happy
- ☐ To feel engaged and not bored
- ☐ To not suffer from physical pain
- ☐ To feel excited/inspired
- ☐ To have friends
- ☐ To feel part of something
- ☐ To be able to unwind after a brutal week
- ☐ To be able to focus and concentrate on important things in my life
- ☐ To lose weight
- ☐ To be seen as funny
- ☐ To appreciate others
- ☐ To have a satisfying sex life
- ☐ To get a reasonable amount of sleep
- ☐ To feel capable of taking on the challenges of each new day

Now, consider these questions:

Did you check at least one item?

When you look at this list, do any of these wants not make sense?

If there were an easy way to achieve the items you selected, would you be interested in it?

These are all basic and reasonable things to want; and these wants and needs are exactly what substances do a great job of providing. Substances offer an answer to the struggles and longings that we all have, and they work well.

Using the same list, how do you think your loved one would answer the question "What does substance use or other compulsive behavior do for me?"

- ☐ Helps me feel less anxious
- ☐ Helps me feel less depressed
- ☐ Makes me feel good/happy
- ☐ Takes away the boredom
- ☐ Lessens my physical pain
- ☐ Makes me excited/inspired
- ☐ Helps me socialize
- ☐ Lets me feel part of something
- ☐ Helps me unwind after a brutal week
- ☐ Helps me focus and concentrate on important things
- ☐ Helps me lose weight
- ☐ Makes me funny
- ☐ Helps me appreciate others
- ☐ Lets me enjoy sex
- ☐ Helps me get to sleep
- ☐ Makes it easier to face the day
- ☐ Other

If you put them in order, which do you think are your loved one's top two reasons for using alcohol or drugs (or other compulsive behavior)?

____

____

You might balk at the idea that your loved one's behavior, which may seem incredibly destructive from the outside, serves a need. Thinking about what your loved one gets from their substance use may be distressing for you. It's worth recognizing that behaviors that may make other people worried, upset, or mad, or that seem unhealthy, are very common. Unhealthy behavior isn't always as extreme as substance use; people with high blood pressure don't exercise, people eat ice cream even though their doctor said to cut back sugar, and people procrastinate even as a deadline approaches. Something must make sense about these choices, despite the negative effects.

The decision to use substances is like any other choice we make: if we choose to keep doing it, it must be working in some way or giving us some feeling that we want, prefer, or need. Understanding what reinforces your loved one's substance use—which reasonable, basic human need the substance use meets—can show you the way forward. And by considering (from their perspective) the positives and negatives of changing versus not changing, you can pinpoint what needs to shift to tip the scale toward change.

It also helps to consider the bigger picture of the behavior. Which people, circumstances, and experiences reinforce the choices your loved one is making? Does anything happen before the behavior that makes it more or less likely to occur? Is anything happening after (consequences) that make it more or less likely to happen again? Putting the behavior in this bigger picture, by considering the before and after, lets you know how to create the conditions to positively influence their behavior in the future.

Putting Behavior in Context with Behavioral Analysis

To practice analyzing behavior in this way, read the following vignette and think about the behavior it describes.

I was with my friends at the park, and someone had a bunch of pills. B. said they were painkillers, and I could tell they were the ones I liked. I know I said I wasn't going to do them anymore, but it was Friday after a lousy week, and I was a bit uptight. School, arguing with my parents, I was pretty down and thought this would be a nice way to take the edge off. I was kind of excited when I saw the pills. I took one and downed it with a beer. I started to feel pretty good, spent the rest of the night listening to music with my friends, laughing, and having a pretty cool time.

Saturday morning, I was bummed that I messed up again *and was nervous that I'd have a urine test. My parents would freak if they found out. I also wound up sleeping late and missed my shift at the restaurant.*

Now, let's list some of the things we could notice.

First, think about what happened before the drug use. What are some of the external events you noticed that may explain why this person did what they did?

____

____

What are some of the of the internal events you noticed?

____

____

Second, think about the outcomes/consequences. What are some of the positives that came out of this person's behavior, from their perspective?

____

____

What are some of the negatives that came out of this person's behavior, from their perspective?

____

____

What did you notice about what happened before the drug use—the antecedents to the behavior? For external events, you might've noticed the fact that the person was at the park; it was a Friday night out with friends; a difficult week; and they saw the pills. For internal events, you might've noticed that they were stressed, feeling upset about the fight they'd had with their parents, feeling down—and then feeling excited when they saw the pills.

And what outcomes did you notice? You likely picked up on some positives—this person felt pretty good when they were using and spending time with friends—and some negatives—that the next day, they were left feeling bummed out again, nervous about the results of the drug test, their parents' reaction, and the prospect of missing work.

This **behavioral analysis** (also known as a "**functional analysis**") that you just completed lets you understand the behaviors of another person by considering what came before and the consequences that followed.

Remember, the strongest reinforcers happen first and fast: the more immediately a consequence follows a behavior, the more powerful the learning experience. If you consider the order of events in this situation, you'll see that drug use yielded immediate positive consequences, while the negative consequences were delayed; in this case, they weren't evident to the person using until the next day.

Now, consider this scenario with a different behavior choice and different consequences.

I was with my friends at the park, and someone had a bunch of pills. B. said they were painkillers, and I could tell they were the ones I liked. I know I said I was not going to do them anymore, but it was Friday after a lousy week, and I was a bit uptight. School, arguing with my parents, I was pretty down and thought this would be a nice way to take the edge off. I was kind of excited when I saw the pills. Then I remembered how my last relapse happened and the trouble it caused. I also thought about how lousy the last detox was. I said "no." After that, I hung out for a bit, but I didn't really feel like I fit in; they were having a good time, so I left and went home. The night was kind of a bummer… I watched TV alone, but I guess I was happy I didn't lapse.

Saturday morning, I was pretty psyched that I didn't use! I went to work and was relieved that I wouldn't get in trouble this week.

As you think about what influenced the decision not to use substances and to go home instead, consider the immediacy of the reinforcement. Were the first consequences the person experienced positive or negative? In terms of timing, the positives mostly occurred the next day. In other words, they were not first or fast. The most immediate consequences were negative, including discomfort, feeling down, and feeling left out. For some people who struggle with substance use—especially if they're still early in the process of behavior change—the fact that the most immediate consequences of the decision not to use are negative might steer them to choose to use.

Learning how to analyze behavior and the contexts in which it occurs—including the triggers that cause it, the consequences that arise from it, and whether those consequences reinforce the behavior—can help you see how your loved one is behaving, and why. This, in turn, is information you can use to be helpful to your loved one and support alternative behaviors and outcomes. In other words, to invite change.

Exercise: Making Sense of Your Loved One's Behavior

To promote positive activities that can compete with your loved one's substance use, you'll need to understand what is reinforcing their current behavior. In this exercise, we guide you to reflect on the circumstances surrounding their use with the table below.

Note: This may be distressing for you. Remember that understanding the reasons for someone's behavior is not the same as agreeing with them, and that acknowledging what makes sense about their behavior can help you help them more effectively. If you're not sure what a question is getting at, you can refer to the example on the next page.

EXAMPLE

BEHAVIOR	TRIGGERS		CONSEQUENCES	
	External	Internal	Short-Term Positive	Long-Term Negative
What does your loved one usually use? Alcohol–wine, cocktails–and sometimes cocaine.	**Who is your loved one often with when using?** Two girlfriends she met at her new job.	**What might your loved one be thinking about before using?** I guess it's some combination of wanting to celebrate what she accomplished at work and to forget about the responsibilities of her job.	**What does your loved one like about using with certain people?** She likes that she feels accepted and celebrated by these colleagues.	**What are the negative results of your loved one's substance use in these areas:**
How much does your loved one usually use? I have no idea and I'm afraid to ask, but enough to drink that she's slurring her words, and enough coke that she doesn't get to bed until 4 or 5 in the morning.	**Where does your loved one often use?** At bars near work. In the bathrooms of bars.	**What might your loved one be feeling before using?** Excited to be with her friends outside of work, celebratory if she had a good day at work, dreading coming home and fighting with me.	**What does your loved one like about where they use?** She likes talking to new people and feeling glamorous and sometimes dancing.	**Relationships** Distance and arguments with me. Drifting from her other friends.
Over how long a period of time does your loved one usually use? 5 – 6 hours, more when she uses coke. 1 – 2 times a week.	**When does your loved one often use?** After work until 1 or 2, later when she does coke.		**What does your loved one like about using?** She says it makes her feel close to her two friends and excited about life. Also confident and powerful.	**Physical health** Tired and hungover the next day, sometimes the next two days.

EXAMPLE

BEHAVIOR	TRIGGERS		CONSEQUENCES	
	External	Internal	Short-Term Positive	Long-Term Negative
			What pleasant thoughts does your loved one have when using? That it's better than eating and watching TV alone (I work late most nights). That she'd rather stay out than come home and feel judged by me.	**Emotional health** Grouchy in the mornings; even more stressed out about work.
			What pleasant feelings does your loved one have when using? Outgoingness, excitement, mischievousness, specialness.	**Legal** She's here on a green card and this could disqualify her from becoming a citizen.
				Financial It costs hundreds of dollars a week to eat out, drink out, and sometimes buy coke.
				Other She stopped playing softball with her old friends.

Now try to complete this exercise using your loved ones behavior.

BEHAVIOR	TRIGGERS		CONSEQUENCES	
	External	Internal	Short-Term Positive	Long-Term Negative
What does your loved one usually use?	Who is your loved one often with when using?	What might your loved one be thinking about before using?	What does your loved one like about using with certain people?	What are the negative results of your loved one's substance use in these areas:
How much does your loved one usually use?	Where does your loved one often use?	What might your loved one be feeling before using?	What does your loved one like about where they use?	Relationships
Over how long a period of time does your loved one usually use?	When does your loved one often use?		What does your loved one like about using?	Physical health

BEHAVIOR	TRIGGERS		CONSEQUENCES	
	External	Internal	Short-Term Positive	Long-Term Negative
			What pleasant thoughts does your loved one have when using?	Emotional health
			What pleasant feelings does your loved one have when using?	Legal
				Financial
				Other

How was that for you? Our hope is that this process of behavioral analysis gives you a bird's-eye view of the triggers, both internal and external, that compel your loved one to engage in the behaviors they do. We also hope it helped to identify the short-term positive consequences that sustain the behavior and the long-term negative consequences that might represent points at which you can intervene and help your loved one change their behavior.

Putting It All Together

We applaud your effort on the previous exercises! Here's a place to sum up what you've learned, as we prepare to move to the next part of understanding: the insight that one size does not fit all, and that you and your loved one should—and can—find a way to change that works for them.

What do you think your loved one gets from using substances? In other words, what are the benefits of their use? Draw from your own observations. Try to avoid judgment ("Because she's impulsive" or "These are not reasons, they're excuses!") and focus on their "why." What effect(s) do they like? In what ways does using a substance seem to help them? What things in their life are enhanced by using and what negative things are lessened? What needs or wants would they have to satisfy in other ways if they were to stop or reduce their substance use?

____

____

____

____

____

____

____

____

List reasons why your loved one may find stopping or reducing their substance use difficult. What might they lose or feel they'll be giving up? (Hint: Some might come from the list of benefits you came up with just now.) What are some potential barriers to initial attempts at stopping?

CHAPTER 2

One Size Does Not Fit All

Understanding that one size does not fit all invites your loved one to find a way to change that works for them.

Addicts are all the same.

You're codependent.

If he doesn't go to rehab, he will die.

She needs to hit rock bottom before she'll listen to reason.

You need to go to Al-Anon.

Common misunderstandings about substance use like these unhelpfully lump together everyone who struggles with substances and assume that the path to change is always the same. We've been saying this for years, and it bears repeating:

> Traditional notions of addiction give you two, and only two, options. People are said to be addicts or not. Addicts are said to be ready to change or not. They're either recovering or they're in denial, "with the program" or not. (In the black-and-white view, there's only one program.) Treatment is rehab or nothing. Success or failure. Healthy or sick. "Clean" or dirty. Abstinent or relapsing. (Foote, Wilkens, and Kosanke 2014)

The list of opposites goes on. "Real" recovery is going to AA meetings every day, getting a sponsor, and working the steps; anything else doesn't count. Treatment professionals and laypeople alike often make generic, blanket recommendations about what a person should be doing "if they really want to change."

Friends and family often find themselves in the same black-and-white world: you're either doing too much or too little, "an enabler" or ready to "get real and use tough love." You may have received advice that begins with the phrase "You need to..." This is a clue that the person is speaking not to you, but to "a family member of an addict": that is, they're speaking to their own idea of what such a person faces and needs. If you're brave enough to ask for input (or sometimes even if you don't ask), people will offer their opinions, advice, and even veiled or explicit criticism that can feel harsh or confusing or fill you with shame and self-doubt. It can also cause conflict within your family if everyone has different emotions and a different opinion on what to do.

Thankfully, these ideas and mandates are not the capital-T Truth, and they're not your only options. In this chapter, you'll explore the one-size-fits-all solutions that you and your loved one might have been given and why they may not have worked. And you'll learn how you can look at your actual situation and your actual needs, as an individual and as part of a family that is dealing with a loved one's struggle with substance use, so that you can come to trust your own knowledge and instincts for what to do next.

A New Perspective on Your Unique Situation

Behavior is complex, and the whys behind one person's actions, or what makes sense to them, may not be the same set of whys for another. In other words, the reinforcers that motivate substance use are different for everyone, and the next person's answers to the exercises in the last chapter could look very different from yours.

It's safe to say that every person who struggles with substances is different, and so are the people who love them. Current scientific evidence tells us that biology, psychology, and social (*biopsychosocial*) contexts influence people's relationship with substances. The reasons for why a person uses substances, as well as for where they fall on the continuum of severity, are a combination of these factors. Some unique combination of these factors also influences how the people who love them behave in response.

Furthermore, the positive reinforcers for change in your loved one will be just as unique as their reasons for using substances. Understanding this is the starting point to identifying those positive reinforcers. There are many ways people can be helped (NIDA 2020) and people can be helped at all levels of use and at any degree of motivation to change (Robertson, David, and Roa 2003; SAMHSA 2019).

We know that forcing people to choose one path or insisting that they think about their problem in a certain way (recall that advice you've been getting) increases the chances of meeting resistance to change (Hadland, Park, and Bagley 2018; Moyers et al. 2007). For instance, insisting that a person admit they are an addict is, for many people, a barrier to change (White and Miller 2007). Staging a confrontational intervention, where the only outcome you're willing to accept is an inpatient rehab program, can make a loved one feel attacked and backed into a corner, and make them more likely to argue or simply refuse (Bien, Miller, and Tonigan 1993; Miller 1985). Strategies like giving people options that make sense to them and that are consistent with their specific needs, resources, and values (like the option to go to an intensive outpatient versus inpatient program), or considering the downsides of their substance use without the stigma of the addict label, get more buy-in and engagement with the change process.

And just as each individual struggling with substances is unique, so are the people who love them. In the same way that each struggling person is guided by a unique set of biopsychosocial factors, families are made up of a group of people with different wants, needs, influences, and values. It turns out that giving families options that are specific to their needs is important. Family members can have a significant positive impact on their loved one's willingness to seek help and reduce their use, and there are many ways they can help. Forcing families to choose one way—like a traditional intervention or "letting him hit rock bottom"—is not effective. Having options is.

Why Understanding That One Size Does Not Fit All Matters

Ultimately, if you're seeking a cut-and-dried response to the question "What should I do if someone I care about is drinking or using drugs?" the answer is that it doesn't exist. The path forward will depend on the makeup of your family as a whole and on your loved one as a unique individual. It will depend on what other challenges you face (individually and together), what substance(s) they're using, how much and how often they use them, how long the behavior has been going on, how old they are, who their friends are and what they think about substances, and a slew of other factors. There are as many ways to change as there are people with a substance-use problem.

As you read the following profiles of loved ones and their family members, you can ask yourself, *Would I make the same recommendation about how to change to all these people?*

- A former soldier with PTSD who drinks to block out her nightmares and yells at her kids when she is drunk. Her husband, who gets really disappointed with her because his father drank too much, is worried about their children.

- An insecure teen who smokes pot before school to fit in with his peer group and is failing his classes. His grandmother is raising him.

- A grieving sixty-year-old who lost her husband to cancer and is over-taking her sleeping pills. Her daughter lives across the country.
- A firefighter who's taking more and more opioids to deal with his chronic pain from falling through the floor of a burning building. His son checks in on him when he can.
- A twenty-four-year-old who uses IV drugs and has an abusive partner who drinks heavily. Her parents each work two jobs to support her three younger siblings.

All these people have unique reasons that their decision to use substances makes sense to them, and the family members concerned about them face different emotional and logistical issues, including finances, time, other life demands, past trauma, and the state of their relationship to the person who's struggling. What would work well for one may not work at all for another, and the same principle applies to you.

With that in mind, let's take a moment to consider the one-size suggestions that you've heard, why they haven't worked, and how you might figure out what will work better for you, your loved one, and your family.

Exercise: The One-Size Suggestions I've Heard

This exercise will help you notice the advice that you get and its emotional impact on you, and give you permission to consult your own knowledge and wisdom as you seek answers and pathways forward.

Read through the examples, then make a list of the advice you've received from other people about how to deal with your loved one's substance use—particularly the comments that trigger self-doubt. Next to each of those triggers, list an alternative thought or coping response. This is an exercise in sifting through the feedback you get, comparing it with your own thoughts, experience, and knowledge of your loved one, and learning to trust yourself.

Feedback/Trigger Comment	Alternative Thought/Coping Response
"You should send her away to rehab."	We can't afford rehab, and I want to help her make changes while she's in her normal life.
"You should kick them out."	We're not willing to kick them out right now—that feels harsh, and we can think of many steps to try before taking such drastic action.
"You should chill out. It's just pot."	I'm concerned because of the changes we've seen: grades dropping, different friends, quitting basketball, seeming to not care about anything.
"Don't trust a word she says!"	I actually have a good connection with her. And while she does lie to me at times, I know she also comes to me when she's feeling down, and I'm not willing to lose that by constantly doubting her.

What did you discover as you completed this activity? Our hope is that you got some clarity about your loved one and your family's situation, and some confidence in your instincts and capabilities when it comes to what to do next.

It's also worth keeping in mind that as your change process unfolds, you may start to notice a similar impulse to give such advice to others. Once you've found an approach that works for you, the desire to help others by "giving them the answer" can be strong. This comes from a place of caring but, remember, one size doesn't fit all; what works well for you and your family won't necessarily serve another person and their family.

Now, armed with the knowledge that (1) behaviors make sense, and (2) one size does not fit all, you can consider your loved one's unique reasons for using and your family's unique situation and challenges, and begin to identify the range of strategies that may be helpful to your loved one and family in trying to change.

Exercise: How Are We Unique?

To identify which paths to change might best fit your situation, it's helpful to first understand the individual strengths and vulnerabilities of your loved one and your family, your unique circumstances and characteristics.

Consider the challenges and strengths of your loved one and your family in each of the following categories.

1. Genetics/family history (e.g., family history of substance use disorder, depression/bipolar disorder)

   Strengths:______________________________

   ____

   ____

   Challenges:______________________________

   ____

   ____

2. Age (e.g., elderly and recently lost spouse, adolescent and extremely impulsive)

   Strengths:____________________________________

   ____

   ____

   Challenges:___________________________________

   ____

   ____

3. Emotional/psychiatric struggles (e.g., trauma, recent death in the family, difficulty expressing emotions, hard time leaving the house because of panic attacks)

   Strengths:____________________________________

   ____

   ____

   Challenges:___________________________________

   ____

   ____

4. School/work (e.g., current lack of direction, high-stress job, negative school environment)

   Strengths:____________________________________

   ____

   ____

   Challenges:___________________________________

   ____

   ____

5. Support of friends/close relationships (e.g., has few friends, friends all use substances, difficulty with intimacy)

   Strengths:____

   ____

   ____

   Challenges:_______________________________________

   ____

   ____

6. Length of time using (there are significant differences between someone who has been using for six months and someone who has been using for over a decade) and different ways of using (oral, nasal, smoking, and intravenous use of substances all have different effects and challenges)

   Strengths:____

   ____

   ____

   Challenges:_______________________________________

   ____

   ____

7. Exposure to treatment (e.g., has had negative experiences previously, likes therapy, is petrified of groups) and openness/engagement in treatment

   Strengths:____

   ____

   ____

   Challenges:_______________________________________

   ____

   ____

8. Finances (e.g., need to consider long-term plan for treatment finances, not just short-term solution)

   Strengths:____

   ____

   ____

   Challenges:_______________________________________

   ____

   ____

Next, zoom out and think about options for change going forward, considering all the factors you've just written about.

9. What are some options for formal treatment that your loved one might consider?

   ____

   ____

   ____

10. What resources outside of treatment might help give your loved one access to new, constructive behaviors or positive emotional support (e.g., community centers, places of worship, free support groups, community elders, etc.)?

____

____

____

____

11. What new behaviors/activities/relationships/pathways could replace old ones?

____

____

____

____

12. What would be challenging for them about adopting any of these new behaviors?

____

____

____

____

13. The ways you help your loved one change have to work for you and your family. What do you foresee as challenges for you and your family?

____

____

____

____

Putting It All Together

Taking your loved one and family's specific circumstances into account together with the reasons they might have for changing or staying the same invites greater ownership on the part of your loved one—which is truly a powerful force of change. This is what we're aiming for! When someone sees that you understand the situation from their perspective—that you recognize both the particulars of their struggle and the options they might actually want to take—they'll be more likely to see themselves in the change process and collaborate with you. They'll be more likely to realize the ways in which they want to change rather than feel put upon by the ways you or others want them to change. And when a person finds reasons that make sense to them to consider doing something new, they're well on their way to change, and that change is more likely to be sustained (Downey, Rosengren, and Donovan 2001).

In part 3, we'll explore strategies for inviting this kind of ownership and collaboration and for supporting positive choices: how to improve family relations and friendships, reinforce healthy habits, and introduce new interests. Treatment and other therapeutic activities can also help, and the various types of treatment are plentiful—some better supported by evidence or more accessible, affordable, or attractive than others. (Our book *Beyond Addiction* has a whole chapter about treatment options.) For now, the main takeaway is this: your family has options, and people respond positively when they can pursue the option that fits them best. On this the evidence is clear.

It helps to realize that there's not only room but also a need for different strategies and paths to change (Miller, Forcehimes, and Zweben 2019). Moreover, understanding the uniqueness of each person involved is a respectful and collaborative place to come from—whether you're a parent, spouse, teacher, nurse, therapist, anyone. The bottom line? Understanding your loved one's uniqueness and giving them options increases their motivation to change.

CHAPTER 3

Ambivalence Is Normal

Understanding that ambivalence is normal invites your loved one to examine their behavior from all sides, to weigh the pros and cons of old and new behaviors and find a balance that actually works for them.

She's obviously not ready yet!

He's a liar. He says he's serious, but he's not.

She started to change, but went back to her old ways. She's in denial!

If they can get away with using again, they will.

They're just making excuses.

Yet another unhelpful attitude about substance use involves a tendency to judge (and perhaps despair over) whether someone is really ready to change. The misunderstanding in all the above statements comes from the idea that a person needs to reach some mythical point of no return, a lightning-bolt moment or level of resolve after which they're all-in on change. From this perspective, there's no room for them ever to be uncertain about the need for change or their ability to manage it. It's an understandable point of view, especially for those whose loved ones have really struggled to change. The good news is, it's not true.

In fact, given that people have reasons for doing what they do, reasons that make sense and matter to them, **ambivalence** about change is normal and to be expected. When we try to give up a behavior that generates something positive for us, there will naturally be some hesitation, some doubt, some ambivalence. Even if in theory we know that there are good reasons to make a change, our reasons for doing things the old way don't simply disappear. The pros and cons of any behavior—and any behavior change—can create a tension that we experience as ambivalence, the feeling of wanting two opposing or conflicting things at the same time. Substance use is no exception. In this chapter, you'll see how ambivalence doesn't mean someone doesn't want to change or is failing at changing. Rather, ambivalence is a natural part of change.

We'll show you ways to deal with the ambivalence about change that your loved one inevitably will experience, and you'll learn tools that can help you persist, with understanding and compassion, when you encounter bumps, detours, or setbacks along the way. As you'll see, with the right understanding, ambivalence can be an opportunity to help someone recommit to change.

A New Perspective on How to Handle Ambivalence

If someone you love is trying to quit or reduce using substances, don't be surprised by ambivalence, or the desire to go back to old ways from time to time. They are not in denial or being stubborn; they're simply remembering what has worked in some way in the past. Learning different behaviors that fulfill a need or provide benefit will eventually help produce and sustain change, but this usually doesn't happen overnight, and hardly ever without the occasional return, or wish to return, to old behaviors. Expect that new habits and lasting change will take time, and that sometimes change will make sense to your loved one; other times it won't. This motivational seesaw is normal; it's how ambivalence gets expressed and is par for the course in virtually any attempt to change—from dieting to ending a relationship to switching careers.

Think about something you've wanted to change about your life (such as exercising more, changing your eating habits, or learning a language), but haven't gotten around to or haven't stuck with. Then, imagine describing this struggle to someone else. Take a minute or two to articulate the problem as you've experienced it, explaining any mixed feelings and motivations you've encountered, as well as any self-critical thoughts you've had.

Now, consider two types of responses that the other person might have:

They tell you why it's important that you change, what could happen if you don't change, and how you could or should go about making the change.

versus

They ask you, What could happen if you don't change? Why is it important to you that you change? What's your most important reason for making this change? How could you go about making the change?

What is the difference in the way these two listeners make you feel? Which promotes in you the stronger feeling of wanting to move forward? Why? Finally, which type of listener do you usually resemble when trying to help someone? Could you imagine taking the second approach if you don't already? Hopefully this reflection helped you relate to your loved one's ambivalence and understand how it can be affected by another person's response.

The Cost-Benefit of Change

When it comes to your loved one's substance use, you might wonder, *How can someone be ambivalent, how can they even think about using, when the costs seem so clear?* Of course, change has its benefits, but the reinforcement someone gets from using substances, or their memory of past reinforcement, is still there each time they return to use or consider doing so. As a result, the temptation to use, to do things the old way, makes sense. Adding to that, to change one behavior pattern or habit, people must learn a new behavior to replace it, and the work involved in learning can be hard and uncomfortable.

We can understand change as a cost-benefit analysis, as illustrated in the tables below. The first table uses the (perhaps less hair-raising) example of changing an exercise routine.

Benefits: Reasons to Exercise/Change
Better health
Increased energy
Doctor will be happy
Feel better about myself
Will save money spent on medication

Costs: Reasons to Not Exercise/Not Change
Feel socially awkward in the gym
Enjoy having extra time at home
Get fatigued and sweaty from exercise
Reminds me how out of shape I am
Don't want to pay for the gym

Let's return to substance use. The next table offers some examples of costs and benefits of use versus change. Your loved one's costs and benefits may be different, and you'll find room to explore those below.

Benefits: Reasons to Stop/Reduce Use (Change)
Better health
Increased energy
Doctor will be happy
Feel better about myself
Will save money

Costs: Reasons to Not Stop/Not Reduce Use (Not Change)
Feel socially awkward in my life
Enjoy having extra alone time at home
Get fatigued from being social
Reminds me how awkward I am
Don't want to pay for therapy

We hope that these examples illustrate the struggle with ambivalence that is common to all change, not just the decision to give up alcohol or other drugs. Now, take a few minutes to write down some of the things that your loved one would identify as the costs (or negatives) of their substance use. Then write down what they'd see as some of the benefits (or positives). (These might be different for different substances.)

Your loved one's costs (negatives) of using	Your loved one's benefits (positives) of using

Next, consider these two questions:

1. Do the positives erase the negatives? For you it's most likely all too clear that even though someone is getting something they like from using substances, this doesn't negate the negatives that also come along with it.
2. Do the negatives erase the positives? This is not a trick question, though it may feel that way because we'd like the answer to be "yes." We want to believe that the bad stuff that comes with substance use will make the person struggling forget the good stuff. But sorry to say, our brains don't work that way! There is no delete-all button to magically erase the option to return to old behaviors or wipe your loved one's memories of what those behaviors did for them. It's helpful to remember this fact when you're upset and wish that someone would never think about using again.

PAUSE BUTTON

It's also helpful to remember that while we don't have a delete-all button in our brains, we do have a pause button—the ability to notice ambivalence, remember that it's normal, and weigh the negatives, positives, and alternatives before we act—that can help us avoid acting in old, automatic ways. Your loved one has this ability to pause, and so do you.

Why Understanding Ambivalence Is Normal Matters

Someone you care about is doing something that has a downside or else you wouldn't be reading this book. Sometimes that downside is small (they're grumpy in the morning); sometimes it's huge (they're at risk of overdosing). You may be reluctant even to think that there could be an upside, let alone to say that out loud to them. People often hope that if they just stay focused on the negatives, they'll "send the right message" and nudge or shove the other person in the right direction. Getting angry and confrontational, riding them harder, and trying to convince them of the "right path" are all options. Unfortunately, they tend to backfire, since a natural reaction to getting pushed is to push back.

Understanding ambivalence not as a red flag, but as a normal part of the change process and as something you can respond to empathetically and flexibly as it arises, can help you in a couple of ways.

First, it can help you tolerate moments when your loved one expresses ambivalence, like hearing them say, "Okay, maybe seeing someone to help me make changes makes sense," followed by "But all my friends use just as much." If you know that ambivalence is normal, you can resist reacting with judgments that set the conversation back and put barriers between you ("Are you crazy? You're a mess and need to stop using now!").

Second, when you see ambivalence and better understand your loved one's reasons for both changing and not changing, you can develop strategies to address the issues that may kick up ambivalence or make the old ways seem attractive. For instance, if they worry about how they'll deal with the pressure of their job without the nightly drinks they rely on to relax, you can help them work through the pros and cons of doing it the old way as well as the pros and cons of trying something new. And you can help brainstorm alternatives to drinking, like having some alone time at home, undisturbed by dinner-making and the kids. Plus, you can plan to not add to the cons of change yourself, say by not bringing up stressful topics for discussion the minute your loved one walks in the door.

We cannot overstate the positive impact that responding to ambivalence with empathy has on communication. If you follow the urge to focus on only one side of the argument—the reasons someone should change—you're most likely setting them up to defend their reasons for not changing (Moyers and Martin 2006). If you react to comments that express uncertainty about wanting to change with arguing, shouting, or lecturing, the other person will most likely argue and shout back, or just tune you out (Miller, Benefield, and Tonigan

1993). And you may miss a chance to hear the person's thoughts, however quiet, about why they do want to change, because you've shut down the conversation.

But if you can see that substance use makes sense in some way (even though you don't like it), you'll better understand why your loved one goes or wants to go back to it even if they also want to change. Then instead of fighting with their ambivalence, you have the potential to influence their behavior by talking about it in a different—more understanding, less confrontational, kinder—way. By acknowledging ambivalence for what it is and avoiding an argument, you contribute to an environment where the other person has more room to reflect on their own reasons for changing instead of defending themself against you. This has the added benefit of removing yourself as a problem. We'll go into this more in chapter 7, on communication tools, but it's not hard to grasp the difference between the following two exchanges—the first of which disrespects and dismisses ambivalence, while the second understands:

You: "What do you mean you don't want to stop? What is wrong with you?"

Them: "A few drinks are not a big deal. You're always on my case. You're such a control freak!" (Slams door.)

versus

You: "I can see you're struggling right now with wanting to drink but also not wanting to drink."

Them: "Seriously. I had a few drinks and it felt so good to forget everything for a few hours. But I don't want to let down my kid. I feel terrible."

In the second exchange, the speaker begins with precisely the kind of empathy and understanding that allows the struggling person to grapple with their own ambivalence—and ultimately, come to reaffirm the benefits in changing, or in this case, a major drawback of not changing. In the first exchange, on the other hand, each speaker ends up stuck on opposite sides and clashing.

You may have trouble letting go of the idea that someone is just making excuses instead of understanding that their behaviors make sense somehow—that for them there are pros to using substances and cons to stopping. This is often linked to ideas like "People who struggle with substance use are just addicts being addicts." And that is exactly the point:

calling a person's reasons for using "just an excuse" or "just being an addict" means we don't accept that those reasons make sense to them. In addition to invalidating their experience, the other problem with this idea is that it gives you no way forward in helping.

If you can keep in mind that all behavior serves a function, and that ambivalence is a natural human response to changing behavior that has served a function, then both these issues will become easier to deal with.

To help you apply this knowledge, take a second to complete the sentence: My loved one's behaviors make sense to them because ________________________________

____

____

Then ask yourself: Can I help new behaviors make sense to them as well, even if the old ones will also still make sense? If yes, what could I try?

____

____

____

____

____

____

Remember, you can create an environment that helps your loved one shift from older, less constructive behaviors to newer, more constructive behaviors. And acknowledging the pros of the old behavior can be as important as celebrating the pros of the new behavior in making that happen. In part 3, you'll find tools to help you communicate your understanding and tools to help tip the scale of ambivalence toward change.

Putting It All Together

As we move forward in the guide, you'll learn how to manage situations in which your loved one is not progressing in a straight line—or maybe not progressing at all. You'll learn to recognize the signals for when they're open to your input and when they're not, or as we like to call them, the green lights and red lights of communication. We'll help you be aware of your reactions to these signals as a starting point and then help you find ways to respond effectively, using communication strategies that lower defensiveness and keep difficult conversations from shutting down (see chapter 7). For now, just try to keep in mind that ambivalence is normal, it is not personal, and your reaction to it can help propel your loved one toward positive change.

Ambivalence Is Normal: A Meditation

Most of us have heard the expression "Change is hard." But why is that?

Even if change is happening for all the right reasons, it requires giving up something that worked at one point, maybe quite powerfully. And while the downsides of that behavior may be screaming "Stop!" the reinforcing effects are still real and may even still be cherished. In that light, it could be said that shifting to something new also includes a loss. And that loss can be scary, sad, confusing, and profound. Understanding this can be an important bridge between you and your loved one as they think about making a change.

Below is the story of one such loss, written by Dr. Kelly Wilson (2017), a psychologist who struggled with substances for a long period as a young man. His meditation on the process of saying goodbye as he shifted to new behaviors is beautiful and heartbreaking, and we include it here (with his permission) to help you understand the intensity of letting go and stepping forward. We hope it encourages you to reflect, when asking someone to change, on just how hard this can be.

This meditation invites you to think about something or someone meaningful to you. If you've lost someone or if a person you care about is particularly at risk for terrible consequences like death, we recommend that you *not* use that relationship for this exercise.

KELLY WILSON'S MEDITATION

If you are [reading this book], then you have contact with people who are struggling, sometimes really deeply, that are stuck, and from the outside, you can look at that and you just say: What? And often from the inside they too are looking at their own behavior and thinking, *What is wrong with me? Why can't I just stop?* I couldn't come up with anything other than I was just broken. This exercise is meant to give you a glimpse into that.

Even if we have never engaged in these kinds of behaviors at all, there is a seed of knowing what happens in the middle of an episode of addiction that can be known by anyone—even if they have never traveled to that place before—if you're willing to sort of drop down into the experience...and perhaps give you a peek at a world that could be important for when you are sitting beside someone—stuck deep—and you are asking them to change.

> *I want to invite you to think for a moment about something in your life that is sweet to you. You could picture something in your life, something you do, or a person in your life that swells your heart. Something that is sweet and beautiful to you. Breathe and take a moment and let yourself see an image of you engaged in whatever that sweetness is. Maybe it's you with someone you love or you in some activity that you love.*
>
> *If you can conjure that image, rotate the image so you could look into your own face in one of those moments of engagement. See if you can look into your own eyes and into that face that has known that [sweetness]. Take a second and allow yourself to just be bathed in that. Just come to rest in that sweetness—and breathe.*
>
> *Next, I want you to imagine that some set of circumstance[s]—and we won't worry what the circumstances are—but some circumstance arises where you know that whatever it is that's sweet to you is killing you and it's killing the people around you who[m] you love. You realize it. You just know, this is killing me and killing the people that I love.*
>
> *Imagine that you had to take one last look and say goodbye. Breathe. Imagine you could just say, "I'm so sorry. I have to go. I have to go." Breathe. Take a moment and just allow all of that experience to just swirl around you. See if you can let go of any effort, and just let it be there. Allow your awareness to return to your breath and notice how it's steady with you all this time, rising and falling.*

Why would we do something like this? It may seem kind of mean or painful to do this exercise. But we are talking about how to say goodbye, what that is like. We can be quick to completely demonize substance use and to demonize the drugs. It's tricky because it's true. They are demons. It's not hard to identify it that way. But here's the thing, it's not *just* a demon.

The thing I know about those days [when I was using] is that if I got just the right combination of drugs and just the right dose, I would get a moment, just a moment, where it was okay to be inside of my own skin, where I could breathe. And so, for some of the people you are sitting across from, when you ask them to let go of substances, you may be asking them to let go of the only peace that they know in the world. That's it. That longing for the moment where you can breathe, that moment of peace—they are not broken to want that. That's what we all want. The part that gets forgotten is the entirely human longing to be able to draw just one free breath. Breath is a good metaphor for this. If you literally couldn't breathe, like you were underwater or something covering your mouth and nose, you might be able to stay calm for a minute, but there would be a moment in there where you would do anything to get a breath. Even if you know the thing that comes after that breath is horrible. In that moment, that breath, it's a human thing. It's that too.

I wouldn't sit with someone new to recovery and romance the high, but I wouldn't encourage them to demonize it either. If people are too quick to demonize substances, you end up with, I think, a brittle recovery. They weren't crazy when they did that any more than a person is crazy to pull their hand away from a flame. They weren't. And sometimes there are circumstances where you make that a goodbye. "I love you, but we have to quit." That one, to me, has more subtlety, more acknowledgment of the richness and fullness of addiction and that hard walk out of addiction.

That little exercise that we just did, I want to hand that off to you as a tool so maybe the next time you get ready to walk into the room with somebody and you are going to ask them to let go of something, if it's time to let go—before you go into the room, imagine that you found yourself in a circumstance where you had to walk away from the sweetest thing you know in this world. Imagine what that moment would be like. How hard that would be. Sit with that for a moment, and then go talk to your loved one. For some people, the ones that are deep into this, you are asking them for something that is that hard. You really are.

PART TWO

Helping with Awareness

In part 1, Helping with Understanding, you worked through some new ways to understand your loved one's behavior. This part, Helping with Awareness, invites you to include yourself in the change process by focusing on your experience. Increasing your awareness of yourself—your emotions, reactions, values, and personal limits—makes a huge difference in being a more effective helper. We often describe this part of helping as "what you can do on the inside" (while the final part of the book, Helping with Action, addresses what you can do "on the outside").

In this part, we encourage you to invite in the difficult parts of the process of helping. We'll help you view your strengths, challenges, and mistakes with more compassion and meet pain with resilience. We'll offer ways to find support, to avoid isolation, and to deal with the effects of shame and stigma. All these things that you can do on the inside create a supportive environment for change, for both your loved one and yourself.

In this part, we ask you to please ask yourself these questions:

- Am I allowed to include myself—my pain, my hopes, my desire to help—in this process?
- As my family experiences pain and struggle, is there also room for kindness, pleasure, and joy?
- As I try to help this person, can I leave room for both of us to make mistakes along the way?
- How do I develop compassion for myself and for them, in my attitudes, thoughts, and behaviors?

By learning to invite in the full spectrum of your experience, you'll stay connected to yourself—how you are and how you want to be—and to everything else that you care about.

Words from a fellow traveler: *In hindsight, I can see I was exhausted all the time and that really had an impact on how I approached my partner. I was just so focused on keeping her safe that I wasn't taking care of myself or staying connected to anything else I care about. That just made me chaotic and resentful. Every day felt like it might be the day something really bad happened. Now, I am trying to do at least one thing a day for myself and it's really helping me keep my balance as I try to help her. Some bad things have happened, but I have dealt with it all okay and I just feel better as a person.*

CHAPTER 4

Self-Awareness Lets You Be You (and Choose Who You Really Want to Be)

Being aware of *you* helps you help *them*; starting there, painful as it may be, brings compassion into your invitation to change, which is an invitation more likely to be accepted.

I feel lost.

If I slow down, I get so depressed.

My partner and I are both so irritable all the time!

It's just relentless.

I can't feel anything but anger. He's such a jerk.

Does any of this sound familiar?

Loving someone who struggles with substance use is incredibly stressful and can affect just about every area of your life. Your concern for them can distract you from your other responsibilities, relationships, social connections, and interests. It can cause you to neglect your own health and sacrifice your financial well-being. Plus, living in constant crisis mode can wear you down so much that you lose patience and resilience. You may doubt yourself and your ability to be a loving family member. It may leave you with a chronic lump in your throat, tightness in your chest, or knot in your stomach.

When someone you care about is using substances, their behaviors will upset you, plain and simple. You may face seemingly endless emergencies and threats that pull you into constant action mode (or ready-for-action mode). You may not even know how you feel anymore—instead, you react automatically to problems as they arise. But what would you find if you were to take a breath and check in with yourself? If you're like many people in this struggle, probably a lot of worry, fatigue, agitation, and uncertainty. Why take time to notice *that*?

Like it or not (and we hope you will grow to like it!), helping a loved one through change is not a one-way street, as the most powerful way to help change occur is to be part of the change yourself. An important step in that process is becoming more aware of yourself.

A New Perspective on Self-Awareness and Change

Self-awareness as we define it in ITC includes checking in on your feelings, your thoughts, your reactions, and your body. Self-awareness also includes realigning yourself with your values: remembering what you care about as a family member and a person, and finding ways to keep those clear in your heart, mind, and actions.

In essence, self-awareness will be the difference between being proactive and strategic versus simply reacting to whatever you face day to day. When you take time to check in with yourself, you're much better prepared to respond to difficulties in an intentional and constructive way instead of shutting down or lashing out, responses that can set both you and your loved one back. Under stress, all too often we lose track of our limits, our emotions, our reactions, and what's really important to us. Increased self-awareness allows for less impulsivity and reactivity, and more responses like these: *I'm way too stressed to be helpful right now* or *It's important to me to keep my cool because I want to help create safety in our home.*

Self-awareness allows you to proactively consider, for instance, how you want to react the next time you feel lied to. You can come up with a plan for that. You might resolve to step away until you're calm enough to respond in a measured, deliberate way. In the moment, you can pause and put that plan into action, instead of hurling accusations and starting a two-day fight. Self-awareness puts space between events and reactions, and that space gives you the chance to respond more effectively, and in accordance with your values.

Exercise: Acknowledging the Hard Parts

Of course, staying connected to yourself, your values, and your loved one while they struggle with substance use is hard. But though it's painful, it's important to pay attention to what's hard about your own experience. If you don't acknowledge the hard parts, or if you try to block them out, it's like taking a road trip in a bad storm and refusing to look at the gas gauge—it's hard enough already, and then you unpredictably run out of gas. But if you see the situation that you and your gas tank are in with clear eyes, you'll know to take the time to fill up before you leave.

So, we invite you to pause and take a moment to notice what about this personal and unique journey you're taking with your loved one is stressful for you. On the following page, write down each item and give it a rating that reflects how difficult it is.

What about helping my loved one is hard for me?	Rate 1 – 5 1 = Bothersome 3 = Difficult 5 = Extremely painful

Once you've completed the exercise, take a second to notice what it was like to allow yourself the room to write about difficulties. Did this feel like a relief? A nuisance? A waste of your time? Not allowed? Did it make you feel guilty? How often do you allow yourself to acknowledge the difficulties you face?

Ultimately, being aware of what you're going through—looking squarely and compassionately at your pain—is key to helping your loved one and yourself along the path to change. The work may be hard, but it's not in vain; it's part of building your awareness skills and becoming part of the change you wish to see.

Present-Moment Awareness: A Starting Point

Present-moment awareness—awareness of your own internal experiences as they happen—allows you to stay emotionally and physically balanced as you address the problems you face.

There are plenty of ways to check in with yourself, including taking a deep breath or two, going for a drive by yourself, meditating or praying, and many other strategies. When you pause to be in the present moment, you'll likely notice the following internal experiences:

- The reality of the situation:

  This is not what I want, but it is what we have.

  I actually can't control this.

  This is not how it used to be.

- Your emotions:

  I feel such a loss—I wanted so much for them.

  I feel ashamed about where our family is.

  I feel overwhelmed.

  I'm furious with him for not trying harder.

  I love her and that hurts so much right now.

- Your thoughts:

  I really don't know what to do.

  Maybe this is because of my bad parenting.

  Something terrible could happen.

  She just doesn't care about anything.

  How can I acknowledge the good parts of what he does with all of this going on?

- Your physical reactions:

  Headaches

  Upset stomach

  Fatigue

  Tension or physical pain

  Tears

- Your actions:

  Avoiding situations

  Yelling

  Skipping dinner

  Not sleeping

  Procrastinating

Though it can be hard, allowing these thoughts, feelings, sensations, and realities into your awareness helps you help them more effectively. You may not feel you have a second to think about these things, but recognizing the level of stress you're under hopefully will inspire you to address it, which will help keep your emotions from boiling over or freezing up.

Many of us spend most of the day at our jobs, running errands, seeking entertainment, or being online. We don't take much time to pause. Does the very idea of pausing make you want to move on to the next page? We get it! But we still encourage you to give it a try.

Creating space—stopping and noticing—takes practice. It includes intentionally choosing to become more aware, having a process that allows you to pay attention, and choosing to remain open to this process and vulnerable to what may come up. In other words, deciding that you're going to do it, how you're going to do it, and why it matters that you do it.

Take a few minutes now to consider some ways you could give yourself room to check in with yourself. We mentioned meditation and prayer. Other examples include practicing deep breathing, going for a walk, taking a bath, or lingering in bed and checking in with yourself before you start your day. Write your ideas here:

____

____

____

____

What could get in the way of any or all of these ways of making room for yourself? How might you deal with these obstacles and check in with yourself on a daily basis, if only for a few minutes? Troubleshoot your ideas here:

____

____

____

____

Once you've found the time and space, check in with yourself in these areas:

- How you're feeling physically: Do you feel pain, fatigue, or changes in your breathing or heart rate?
- How you're feeling emotionally: Are you feeling more of anything (sad, afraid, weepy, angry, impatient)? Are you feeling less of anything (content, peaceful, optimistic)? Are you numb or checked out?
- The thoughts you're having: Are you thinking things like, *This is not how it should be, What have I done wrong?* or *Will this ever end?* Do these thoughts lead to other emotions, like guilt or shame?

- The actions you're taking: Are you avoiding others, becoming tearful, losing your temper, sleeping or eating more or less than normal? Are you drinking more than you want or using other substances?

Be gentle with yourself as you ask these questions. We're only asking that you notice yourself in some of these ways. As painful as it might be, it's a great and important start! Without it, you cannot learn to create space between the pain and your reactions, which lets you respond to your loved one's struggles in the way you want. (See our online resources for another meditation to help you pause and create space for yourself. And later, in the chapter on self-compassion, we'll help you use this awareness to take better care of yourself, which can also have a positive impact on them and their ability and willingness to change.)

Your Values: What Matters to You

The second part of self-awareness takes you beyond the present moment to your values, or what matters most to you. When you're getting walloped by the consequences of someone else's choices, it can be hard to see that person's redeeming qualities or to feel any desire to stay connected to them. It may even seem easier to sever all ties. However, before you do anything that might shatter the relationship, we recommend that you pause and reconnect with what matters to you in your life and in your relationship with your struggling loved one. This might run counter to what others in your life are saying to you.

Connecting to what matters to you is the anchor, or the why behind wanting to help. Take a moment to consider these questions:

When you think about your loved one, in what ways do you notice the care you feel for them, even as you feel anger or a desire to disconnect?

____

____

____

____

____

When your loved one says something that might be hurtful to you, can you see past that to why it is important to you to stay connected to them?

____

____

Can you focus your attention on the parts of them that you love and care about? What are those parts?

____

____

____

____

What types of interactions with them feel fulfilling or pleasurable to you, even if they were only in the past?

____

____

____

____

Can you notice the hopes you have for them, in spite of the temptation to give up?

____

____

____

____

Ultimately, the question to keep in mind is, can you reconnect with the parts of this person that you love and with your wish for them to be healthy and well?

What came up as you considered these questions? Many people focus so much more on daily struggles that they stop noticing the hope, love, and enjoyment their loved one can inspire. But those qualities—the caring, the connection, the love—are central to what we cherish, value, and desire most deeply. It's easy to lose track of these things that matter so much. Awareness and, in the next chapter, willingness are how you reclaim them.

You may have noticed that allowing those desires back in kicks up the pain of having those deeply valued things threatened. And it's true that being aware of what we care about opens us up to pain. The possibility of loss, of things that we care about not going well, of wanting deeply and not getting, all are possible when we're vulnerable in this way.

As you work in the next chapters to deal with this pain—to bring it with you as you work with your loved one to change—it's important to check back with yourself about who you are and who you want to be. This can sustain you even when change is painful. Below are some exercises to help you get in touch with just that.

Exercise: Imagining What Really Matters

Imagine you're at your eightieth birthday celebration. Really let yourself sit back with eyes closed and take in the scene as your family and friends gather to honor you and speak about your impact on them.

How would you want your loved ones/friends to talk about you and remember your life? What qualities would you want them to remember lovingly? What impact on their lives would you like people to describe?

____

____

____

____

____

Stay in that same eightieth birthday scene for a moment and picture your loved one who's currently struggling with substance abuse being there:

How would you want your loved one to describe your presence during this period of their life, when they were struggling with substances? What qualities would you want them to remember lovingly? What impact on their life during that time would you like them to describe?

____

____

____

____

As you struggle with your loved one and their substance use, how connected do you feel with that "you" being lovingly and gratefully honored at your eightieth birthday?

____

____

____

____

What would you need to do today to start to become more like that honored person?

____

____

____

____

Think about a recent interaction with your loved one about something difficult (substance use, lack of truthfulness, etc.). Did you respond in a way you liked? How did that make you feel about yourself? How would you rather feel? How would you need to act to feel that way in the long run? What response would have better reflected the qualities you want to bring to your role as a partner/parent/friend/family member? What are those qualities that are most important to you?

____

____

____

____

Putting It All Together

Doing things differently—in this case, starting to let yourself notice *you*—requires stepping out of what you know...and most of us hate that! As you increase your self-awareness, you may start to notice how hard this is to do. You might think, *I'm terrible at this* or *This is really hard to stick with.* You might feel unsure of yourself, awkward, a bit unsteady. These experiences are all to be expected, and they will also happen for your loved one when they start to make changes. Awareness and acceptance of the difficulty of change will create an environment in which everyone feels capable of trying new things. Awareness and acceptance of the difficulty of change will also help you and your loved one tolerate the discomfort that comes with change, including the discomfort of making mistakes, since that discomfort is in the service of something important.

In the next chapter, we'll continue helping you develop your ability to notice what's happening now and do things differently, by teaching you the skill of willingness—being willing to approach what matters, even when it's painful.

CHAPTER 5

Willingness Is a Different Way to Relate to Pain

Willingness is an invitation to yourself—"Are you willing to allow for the vulnerability and pain that come with caring?"

I seem to be numb a lot.

I can't stand feeling this way.

It's not supposed to be like this.

I have not been the parent I want to be.

It hurts my heart to think about it. I'd rather be at work.

As you practice awareness of your experiences and your values, you may notice that your caring and your pain are connected. In fact, they're inseparable. You hurt because you love. You're frustrated because something is in the way of realizing something that matters to you. Your values and what's hard about this are two sides of the same coin.

On side one: what you value in your relationship with this person, including what's important to you about helping them, the care and hope you feel for them, and what you value for yourself as a parent or partner or friend or person.

On side two: vulnerable, uncomfortable, or painful emotions (including fear, hopelessness, anger, and fatigue) that you experience as part of the struggle of caring about and staying connected to someone with substance problems.

Spend some time imagining the two sides of your coin. On the first side: what is important to you about helping your loved one, or why is helping important to you as a person? On the second side: what are the difficult feelings and experiences that arise when you help? You can refer to the exercises in the previous chapter for help. The questions you answered in "Your Values: What Matters to You" (page 72) represent the first side of your coin, and your answers to the exercise "Acknowledging the Hard Parts" (page 67) represent the second.

It's true. You experience pain on this journey because you care. With awareness of why you care, you can choose to stay anchored to what's important to you, even in the face of that pain. This is **willingness**.

A New Perspective on What to Do with Pain

It's human nature to want to avoid pain or make it stop, and we all have our ways of trying to gain control over discomfort. These might include attempts at controlling the other person—for instance, monitoring and controlling their behavior because it helps relieve your fear or anger; or attempts at controlling ourselves, say by shutting down and avoiding your loved one because seeing them causes you heartache. The problem is that these control strategies are usually not very successful, or at least not for very long. And, fighting to keep painful thoughts and feelings at bay takes a toll. While shutting down or trying to control the situation are understandable responses to your loved one's struggle, they each have a downside.

When you attempt to control yourself by shutting down, you risk sacrificing the relationship completely, as the distance grows. When you try to manage your fear or pain by controlling someone else, you set yourself up for anger or disappointment when it doesn't work. Additionally, attempting to control another person often leads to arguments and anger, which can lead the person to point to your reactions as the source of the problem instead of examining their own choices. In the end, both types of control strategies can leave you exhausted, distrustful, anxious, and angry, and can make you want to give up helping entirely.

Willingness is a different path from these controlling strategies. It's choosing to accept all your feelings—even the painful ones—because they allow you to stay connected to what you care most about. This decision to invite in and allow the pain, without chasing it away, is a powerful (though difficult) step, and gives you two big benefits:

1. It helps you stay connected to your loved one and work toward effectively supporting them.

2. It allows you to stay connected to your values—what matters most to you in your relationship and as a person.

And we're back to the coin: on one side, your desire to be connected, compassionate, loving, and helpful to your loved one; on the other side, the despair, fear of failure, and upset that come with witnessing and being a part of the struggle. They can't be separated. If you want to help effectively, you'll need to be willing to pick up the whole coin.

Why Willingness Matters

We are *not* asking you to embrace pain as a test of your strength or determination. We are also *not* suggesting you just "suck it up" in order to help. Instead, we invite you to be aware of the things you value and to stay connected to them as you experience some of the hardship that comes along with caring and change. By understanding that your pain is connected to your hopes and values, you can start to relate to pain in a different way, to realize that it has purpose and meaning. The pain is a clue that you're in the right territory, where you really care and things really matter. In this way, willingness changes meaningless suffering into meaningful suffering.

What does it look like to be willing, to pick up the whole coin? It can look like any of these:

- Trying new things to help your loved one even though part of you wants to give up
- Working to make things different while being angry about the way they actually are
- Continuing to work on your communication skills despite your loved one screaming at you
- Taking better care of yourself while the chatter in your mind says you're being selfish

What do these examples have in common? They're paths to pursuing what matters at a deeper level to you, instead of responding in the moment to the flood of emotions. This is what a true and sustainable invitation to change looks like; it's about change for both of you, not just an attempt to get your loved one to act differently.

The following is an example of a parent's willingness in action.

What happened: *We gave our son his car back after two months without it because of drinking. He came home drunk last night and fell asleep in the car in the driveway, then tried to hide it.*

The coin: *On one side of the coin is what matters to me, my child's safety and increasing communication between us. On the other side of the coin is what is uncomfortable for me, remembering past times of being betrayed and hurt and feeling scared for his safety.*

The willingness choice:

Putting down the coin—If I want to try to make my pain go away, I can lock him out of the house and let my anger rip by telling him he's an untrustworthy liar and shutting down. The problem is while my anger lets me feel less hurt and scared in the short term, he'll hide what he's doing, and by calling him names we have less communication and connection.

Picking up *the coin—If I pursue what matters to me, I can wait until he's clear-headed and I'm calm to sit down to talk about what happened. I can let him know calmly that we're taking the car again for safety reasons, that it's painful to have him unsafe and lying, and that we're stumped as to how to help and need his input. What I've noticed is that this path doesn't give me the short-term relief of yelling, but it leaves things more open for a discussion about realistically helpful next steps. And it lets him know what is so hard about this for us, without injuring anyone emotionally, which matters a lot to me.*

Here, you can see how the willingness to pick up the coin involves change on the part of both the parent and, potentially, the child. You can also see the avenues for change it makes possible. While of course no change is guaranteed—the child's behavior possibly will be the same either way—picking up the coin allows the parent to stay in contact with what they value and be more of the person they want to be.

Willingness Is a Choice—Not an Obligation

As we've acknowledged again and again (and will again), trying to help your loved one will be painful, scary, time-consuming, and uncomfortable at times. It may help you to keep in mind that being willing to pick up the coin is a choice. It is not an obligation; it is not the right thing to do; it is not a badge of really caring. And while it will keep you connected to yourself and them more effectively, it is also hard, and you will be pulled to put the coin down sometimes. In the long run, acting in ways that honor your values will create greater resilience, joy, and connection, but there will be times when you decide to distance yourself from the negative emotions and pain of the moment. We invite you to allow room for these times when you perhaps shut down, zone out, step back, disconnect. If you can do this without the extra weight of berating yourself or shoving all your emotions away, all the better. Allow yourself this choice and the freedom to be human.

There's an expression—"Perfect is the enemy of good." In that spirit, we also hope you'll allow yourself to be willing in small ways, and not think of willingness as a dramatic, earth-shaking, seize-the-day event. Small steps (*I'm going to back off in this moment and not yell*) are the building blocks of real change.

Willingness also applies to you and your own efforts to change. As you practice using the tools in this guide—and inevitably fumble, then practice some more—we encourage you to keep these questions in mind: *Am I willing to give these methods a try even though it's hard and uncomfortable? Do I want to choose willingness here in this moment?* The answer can of course be no, and there are times when it will be no. You might intend to talk with your loved one about a lie they told because you value listening and communication—only to stop listening, yell, and end the conversation instead. You're human, and fumbles like this will be part of the learning process. But giving yourself another chance to practice responding in ways that honor your values will improve your odds of creating an environment of awareness, willingness, and patience in which both you and your loved one can make positive changes.

Exercise: Taking the Path to What Matters

In this exercise, you'll look at some common arguments you have with your loved one to determine the instinctive, make-it-stop reactions you have that might suggest an agenda of controlling your loved one's behavior, and to think about how you might like to show up differently, with willingness to experience pain and move toward what you value and the kind of person you want to be.

When challenging situations arise with your loved one, what make-it-stop reactions do you have? We suggest you take stock of:

- Your thoughts: e.g., *I'm playing that old tape again—"He's doing this on purpose"*
- Your physical reactions: e.g., *My chest is tight with anxiety, My face is flushed with embarrassment, My blood pressure is going up with this tension*
- Your emotions: e.g., *I feel really angry, I'm so disappointed*
- Your behaviors: e.g., yelling, slamming doors, leaving the house, staying in bed all day, or not eating

My make-it-stop reactions (including what I think, what I feel in my body and my mind, and how I behave):

____

____

____

____

Now, take a moment to think about your values as a person and helper. Remember and review what matters to you in your relationship. This could include connection, cultivating a loving relationship, being consistent and reliable for your loved one, keeping them safe, or mutual respect. Which of these values might you be falling short of practicing when you leap to make-it-stop reactions in stressful moments with your loved one?

____

____

____

Finally, we'll ask you to consider potential moments of choice you might have missed in your argument with your loved one. Were there moments when you could have behaved differently? Chosen a different path?

____

____

____

In general, when you encounter these moments of choice, what responses besides your make-it-stop reactions can help you move toward what you care about with your loved one, rather than moving away? These could be new ways to listen and talk to your loved one (chapters 7 and 8), new ways to help reinforce positive choices (chapter 9), or new ways to take care of yourself even when things are hard (chapter 6). Write some ideas down here.

____

____

____

____

Note: A path that increases connection and moves you closer to what matters is not necessarily a path that is less painful in the moment!

Willingness Meets Practice

Choosing willingness takes practice. With practice, you'll see these moments of choice more clearly, and your values—rather than your pain—can guide your actions. Learning to hit pause will help you start from a calm, grounded place, rather than from a reactive place where everything feels like an emergency.

Of course, making the choice of whether to pick up the coin can be difficult in real time. But the basic technique isn't difficult—and it's worth taking some time to familiarize yourself with it now, so you have it ready when you're in a more stressful situation. You already laid the groundwork in the last chapter, with awareness.

Exercise: New Responses to Old Triggers

It's worth thinking about some of the behaviors your loved one does that set you off and planning some responses you might want to try instead of your usual make-it-stop ones. Write those behaviors down in the left-hand column of the chart below. Then, in the right-hand column, plan an alternative coping response.

Trigger	Response
They come home obviously under the influence.	**Old Response:** Standing at the front door and yelling about how irresponsible they are. **New Response:** This week, I'll practice resisting the urge to talk to them when they come home under the influence; instead, I'll go to a place in our home where I don't see them and where I can focus on something else.
They ignore me/take a snotty tone with me when I ask how their day went.	**Old Response:** I take a snotty tone back and say something hurtful. **New Response:** This week, I'll go in my room, relax, and tell myself I can talk to them more effectively tomorrow when I'm calmer.
They bombard me with nasty calls and texts and won't stop until I respond.	**Old Response:** I keep texting back and forth late into the night (losing sleep). **New Response:** I remind myself that I don't have to respond when they're treating me this way. I also know if they're angry or agitated, now probably isn't the best time. I'll send one text telling them I'll talk tomorrow when they're in a better frame of mind.

Your examples:

Trigger	Response
	Old Response: **New Response:**
	Old Response: **New Response:**
	Old Response: **New Response:**

Finally, choose one new response to practice this week.

Whatever your loved one says in the heat of the moment, it's probably safe to trust that they care that you care. Staying grounded and connected lets the other person know that you care and are prepared to stay the course. As you start to develop your pause button—for example, to recognize when you need to take a few deep breaths before responding—and to be aware of what's happening in your head and heart (*Wow, I'm incredibly hurt by her comments and I'm about to be nasty, I can feel it*), you'll increasingly be able to avoid knee-jerk reactions, which can often take you further away from what matters to you.

PAUSE BUTTON: PICKING UP THE COIN

We suggest finding a pause button: a way to stop and listen to yourself, to check in with your values and goals when you find yourself in the middle of a tense or chaotic interaction, or even before you reach that point. Your pause button could look like this:

1. Slow down, and notice where you are and what you're doing. Notice what you're thinking. Notice what you're feeling emotionally and physically and how you're behaving, such as shutting down or trying to exert control.
2. Take a breath. Step away for a moment so you can gather yourself and your thoughts.
3. Remember what matters to you about your loved one and your relationship. Remember what kind of person you want to be in this moment.
4. What could you do now that would lead you closer to being that kind of person?

Putting It All Together

Of course, this is all easier said than done, so here are some tips for managing your emotions, to give you room to choose willingness, even in the heat of the moment. (Some of them—like compassion, self-care, communication, and setting limits—we will discuss in detail in the chapters to come.)

- Anticipate when your challenging emotions are most likely to show up. What triggers your anger, yelling, and other emotions and behaviors? Make a list. Are there particular times or environments where you're more likely to be reactive? Practice your new responses from the trigger exercise above.

- Consider ahead of time what's at stake. Think about the last time you responded to a difficult situation by breaking down, being confrontational, or detaching. You likely felt worse, not better, for losing control or saying things you regretted. Your loved one likely framed your behavior as the problem ("My mom's a nightmare," "My partner always overreacts") and they even may have turned to substances to cope with the negative feelings. This is not to blame you for their actions—rather, we want to help you remove yourself from their reasons for using as well as lessen your stress and anxiety.
- During a heated moment, describe to yourself what is happening and label your feelings, e.g., *I got angry really fast when he used that disrespectful tone with me.* Simply narrating to yourself what's happening can put a bit of distance between you and your reaction.
- Take a time-out. Give yourself permission to avoid the most triggering situations while you try to improve the climate in your home.
- Imagine your loved one is your neighbor's child/spouse/family member/friend, not yours. How would you react? Probably less judgmentally and more calmly, right? Think of a heated situation that often happens with your loved one and try on this perspective for a couple of minutes to see if it helps you get through the moment. What would you advise a friend who was in a similar situation?
- Set a limit. If, upon reflection, you choose not to put up with a particular behavior (such as name-calling or swearing, yelling, or physical aggression), decide ahead of time what the consequences will be and use the communication tools and limit-setting strategy in part 3 of this guide to explain this to your loved one in advance (see chapter 9).
- Take care of yourself. At a minimum, do what it takes to keep up your resilience—get enough sleep, eat a balanced diet, exercise, go easy on the caffeine. All or any of these will help. In addition, ask yourself how you can make time for yourself,

time for activities you enjoy, time with people who make you laugh and feel loved. Read the next chapter for more on self-care (and *Beyond Addiction* for even more).

- Responding in a calm, less confrontational way does not mean passively accepting risky or problematic behavior. It means you're setting the stage for the other person to hear you, to think about their actions, and most importantly, to be more open to trying healthier behaviors (see chapters 7 and 8).

Remember, willingness to have your feelings and act according to your values takes practice. You and your loved one will face setbacks. They may lie to you, be disrespectful, or return to substance use after stopping for a while. You may act in ways you wish you wouldn't, maybe because you feel depleted and willingness in the present moment is escaping you.

Here's where our next chapter—learning to develop self-compassion as part of this whole process—comes in. Change is hard; it takes time—for everyone—and the stakes are high. So, take a breath, be kind to yourself, acknowledge the good you're trying to do and the love you feel, and get back in there!

CHAPTER 6

Self-Compassion Goes the Distance

Self-compassion brings kindness and care to you, to sustain you through an invitation to sustainable change in your loved one. Taking care of yourself also invites them to do the same.

My kid comes first. I'll take care of myself once I get him into treatment.

I don't even want to see friends anymore.

I can't control myself, I keep crying and I feel so weak.

I can't imagine what other people think.

If only I had.../If only I hadn't...

If you love someone with a substance problem, feelings like worry, anger, fear, frustration, helplessness, and shame probably consume some or a lot of your time and energy. Your mind might be full of negative chatter–telling you how you've failed in your role, offering harsh judgments about your record as a parent/partner/friend/family member, or obsessing over the judgment and criticism of others. This all takes a toll on your mental and physical well-being.

The antidote to this is **self-compassion**. You may have the impulse to roll your eyes and move on to the next part of the book, Helping with Action, because you want to get on with doing something about the problem. We get it! It can be really hard to think about your own needs when someone you care about is struggling. That said, we hope you allow yourself to slow down and keep reading, as the evidence tells us that treating yourself with compassion really does help in any process of change (Neff and Faso 2014; Neff, Kirkpatrick, and Rude 2007). We cannot stress enough: helping yourself is part of helping someone else. In this chapter, you'll learn exactly what self-compassion is and how to begin practicing it to bolster yourself as you move into the action phase of ITC. We'll also take some time to deal with a particularly non-self-compassionate emotion, shame, because it's as toxic to you as self-compassion is helpful and sustaining.

A New Perspective on Self-Compassion

Self-compassion helps you find and sustain the willingness to hang in there and pursue your deeper values in the face of pain. It puts safe, healing space between you and those moments when you feel you just can't deal with the heartache anymore. It gives you endurance over the long run. And it models the compassion you'd like to see your loved one practice as they try to change.

But what exactly do we mean by self-compassion, and what does it look like in action? Dr. Kristin Neff, a researcher who studies the subject, outlines three specific ingredients for practicing self-compassion (Neff 2003): mindfulness (what we call self-awareness), as opposed to getting stuck in your feelings and thoughts; self-kindness, as opposed to self-judgment; and common humanity, as opposed to isolation. Let's look at each of those now.

Mindfulness, or self-awareness. You've already learned about one of the components of self-compassion: self-awareness, which Neff and her colleagues call mindfulness. Whatever you choose to call it, it involves making room for all your thoughts, feelings, and bodily sensations, including the painful ones. Self-compassion researchers likewise suggest that you allow for these experiences and notice when you get stuck on building them up or downplaying them in your mind. The goal is to let yourself have your experiences without exaggerating, minimizing, or staying fixated on the hard stuff. In other words, trying to be there in the present, trying to allow each experience or feeling you may be having, and trying not to get them tied up with the past or the future. This kind of awareness, too, is an act of self-compassion. You notice what's happening to you, and you don't rush to judge it or get rid of it. And this inevitably helps you feel better and act with more clarity and purpose. As we've seen, self-awareness or mindfulness is available to you whenever you need it. It's also something that many wise people have taught and written about as a daily practice. You'll find a few of our favorite resources at the end of this book.

Self-kindness. Have you ever noticed the voice in your head that focuses on your shortcomings and mistakes? It tends to be critical and unforgiving and doesn't consider the bigger picture: the difficult circumstances you face as you try to help your loved one. This voice uses fear and shame as motivators, which can work in the short run, but wear you down over time. And successful changes in behavior do take time.

Practicing self-compassion begins with how we speak to ourselves. A voice of self-kindness has a supportive and caring tone. It's tender toward your suffering, helps you get up after failing, encourages you, and gives you space to try again after making mistakes. It reminds you of your loving and generous qualities as a parent or spouse or friend, your willingness to extend your heart even when it feels vulnerable to do so. It uses respect and love as motivators, which can sustain you through a longer journey.

Cultivating a kinder internal voice may not come naturally, especially in difficult moments, but it will strengthen and speak more readily as you practice. Let's take a closer look.

Take a moment to think about a mentor/teacher/coach/boss who *did not* have a positive impact on you (someone who made you feel bad about yourself, less than, or doubtful of your talents). List adjectives and behaviors that describe that person.

____

____

____

Next, think about a mentor/teacher/coach/boss who *did* have a positive impact on you (someone who helped you step into the world, learn new things, take a chance, or feel better about yourself). List adjectives and behaviors that describe that person.

____

____

____

____

How often do you speak to yourself with the helpful mentor's voice versus the not-so-helpful mentor's voice?

____

____

____

____

____

When you think about your interactions with your loved one, how much time do you spend in the positive mentor role versus the not-so-helpful mentor role? How does it feel when you take on each of these roles? What's one thing that you could practice that might be a little bit closer to the helpful mentor role?

____

____

____

____

Common humanity. Another part of self-compassion is how you view yourself in relation to others. Do you let yourself be human, with all the struggles, confusion, tragedy, joy, and hopefulness that come with it? Do you let yourself make mistakes, lose your way, and say the wrong thing, while doing the best you can? Or do you hold yourself to a standard of perfection that leaves no room to make mistakes? Do you compare yourself to others and assume they're doing a better job managing their lives?

It's not uncommon to feel alone and full of shame and blame when struggling with stigmatized problems such as substance use issues in your family. We know you may worry about privacy, gossip, and public perception or judgment. You may feel protective of your loved one or, frankly, embarrassed at times. You may feel shame around things you've done. These feelings can easily lead you to pull away from the support systems you normally rely on. Or you may not be in the habit of asking for help—you may even be dead set against it.

While these are reasonable concerns and valid feelings, isolation can make you feel worse over time, depriving you of the energy and resilience that you need to cope—and to help. Do not underestimate how detrimental isolation can be. It can exacerbate depression, anxiety, and stress, making it more difficult for you to handle emotionally charged situations. Over time, when you're isolated, your emotional resilience shrinks, and your ability to take an emotional hit from your loved one's behavior without sinking or reacting badly yourself significantly diminishes.

The truth is, while your path is unique, millions of people have walked down similar roads and had similar realizations, experiences, heartbreaks, and successes. Some of their experience will look, sound, and feel a lot like what you're going through. We recommend talking to people who share your experience, since research has found time and again that social support helps when it comes to, well, pretty much everything (Ozbay et al. 2007; Reblin and Uchino 2008).

Let's take a moment to consider your social circle, and the sources of compassion in your life. Odds are there are some, even if it doesn't always feel that way, or if you don't always feel you can or want to trust them with your struggle. Take a second to identify people in your life who fill different needs for you. (Some people may fit into more than one category.)

Good listener:	
Good advice giver:	
Fun/makes me laugh:	
Cheerleader/ encourages me:	
Confidant:	
Playmate/likes to do things with me:	
Interesting conversationalist/ gets me talking about other things:	
Shoulder to cry on:	

Fighting the pull toward isolation will help you feel better, and help you help better. And as you work to develop self-compassion, you may find that the compassion of others strengthens and heals you.

Self-compassion is not about pampering yourself or forgetting your troubles; it means being aware of your needs and developing a sense of kindness, respect, and understanding toward yourself. Self-compassion lets you feel part of a larger whole and allows for encouragement, support, and hopefulness. It gives you permission to care for yourself and to make room for things that matter to you (such as your health and other relationships), which in turn helps you help others. It broadens your perspective to see beyond tough moments with your loved one. The world is still going on, and you're still in it.

Here are some examples of self-compassionate responses to the struggle:

- If you lose your cool when you haven't been sleeping well, you can try to go to bed earlier.
- If you're frantically doing things all the time to fend off feeling sad, you can work on giving yourself permission to feel, even if that means crying in the shower until you're more comfortable sharing your tears with others.
- If you're pacing the floor and battling the critical chatter in your mind, you can turn your attention to people or situations that support you.
- If you notice that shame or embarrassment is causing you to isolate, you can try to connect to other people you care about, counteracting the instinct to withdraw.

Ultimately, self-compassion unifies self-awareness (of your own needs, pain, and avenues for connection to the people and things you care about) and willingness (to accept the pain that comes along with caring). Self-compassion will ward off mindsets like *I can't take this* or *Nothing I do works, I give up.* The job of helping can be taxing, but if you build in moments of joy, relief, rest, or comfort, you'll be a more effective helper. You may be surprised that, along the way, you make dear friends who understand you and offer support without judgment, or that old relationships deepen.

Of course, it can be hard to break a pattern of berating and neglecting yourself if it's been in place for a while. If self-compassion doesn't come naturally to you, you're not alone. (Hey, common humanity!) It takes practice.

Exercise: Identifying Roadblocks to Caring for Yourself

This exercise is meant to heighten your awareness of how hard it can be in practice to take care of yourself. Ask yourself, *What derails me from self-care?*

Imagine bumping into a friend at the supermarket who knows that you and your loved one are going through struggles around substance use. They say, "I'm not an expert in addiction, but when I was taking care of my father with dementia, I realized how important it was to give myself some time off to refuel and feel like a human again. You might want to think about that." After you nod and say thanks, in what ways do you react to this advice? Can you notice ways you may set aside their support or discount it? Below, list the thoughts, emotions, and events that have gotten in the way of self-care in the past.

My thoughts (e.g., *I'm secondary in this emergency*; *I appreciate that they care, but they don't really understand my situation*)

____

____

____

____

____

____

My emotions (e.g., fear, shame, anger, despair)

____

____

____

Events (e.g., arranging treatments, monitoring drug use, fighting with my loved one)

____

____

____

____

____

Now that you've identified some of your reactions that derail self-compassion, let's consider some self-care options:

- The possibility of using the pause button to choose a path toward what matters to me
- What my favorite mentor might suggest to me at this moment
- Some self-reflection on the qualities that I value in myself
- Reaching out to someone I appreciate connecting with

We've already looked at the first two bullets in this list in previous sections; later in this chapter, we'll explore specific ways to reach out to people you want to connect with. For now, let's look at the aspects of yourself that you appreciate and value.

Exercise: Appreciating You

Just as we all have imperfections, we all have qualities to be proud of—and self-compassion means appreciating the strengths you possess. In this exercise, try to list ten qualities that you appreciate about yourself. If you get uncomfortable, remind yourself that you're not claiming to be perfect or better than anyone else. You're simply noting the good qualities that you sometimes display. We added a few prompts to help you get started.

1. A personality trait (that I appreciate or think others do)...	2. An achievement...
3. A skill that I feel good at...	4. Something in my life I feel proud about...
5. How I show love or appreciation to others...	6. How I interact with others...
7.	8.
9.	10.

Was it at all a struggle to come up with items to list? Did you find yourself making caveats?

Shame: A Special Case for Self-Compassion

As you completed the previous exercise, did you notice perhaps a sense of shame, for one thing or another, surface? Shame is a common and particularly brutal emotion that can arise for you—the loved one of someone struggling with substance use—as you begin to practice self-compassion. In fact, shame is the opposite of self-compassion, and self-compassion is the best medicine for shame.

Sometimes it's a small nagging voice, sometimes it's a thundering judgment; either way, this "bad, soul-crushing feeling" (as one parent described it) may well be on repeat in your head: *It's me, this is my fault, there must be something wrong with me/my family.* There are many versions of this internal dialogue:

Other people's kids turned out fine…

If I'd only been more (or less)…

I shouldn't have allowed…

How could we have let her (or not let her) be put on those medications?

Why didn't I say something, why didn't I do something, when I first saw something was wrong?

When a loved one is struggling with substance use, it's normal to rethink paths you've taken. Feeling regret about all the pain you and your family are in is also natural. When these feelings turn into shame, however, you've landed in a place that is neither deserved nor helpful, and it takes time and work to defuse the thoughts that have led you there.

Unfortunately, shame is also one of the main reasons people are reluctant to seek help—and for many issues, too, not just struggles with substance use. Shame is a complicated, intensely uncomfortable, and sticky (hard-to-shake-off) emotion. It can be a response to feeling that you've either done wrong or reacted badly. It can include feeling exposed, vulnerable, unsure, or humiliated; it has many sharp edges that make you feel like hiding, attacking yourself, and shutting down. And in the end, shame leaves you with the sense that you are shameful. In contrast to the dull ache of regret, shame is piercing; it makes teasing apart what you've done well and what you might do differently almost impossible, as it puts all your emotions, thoughts, and actions through the same grinder and labels them bad, unforgivable, and your fault.

A Special Note to Parents: While shame is usually triggered by one's own thoughts or actions, having kids makes you vulnerable to a whole other level of shame. For most parents, their children are an extension of their heart and soul. Your child's behavior, attitudes, and experiences expose you to feeling shame for them, about them, and about yourself. On top of that, feeling ashamed of feeling ashamed about your child adds extra insult to injury. This is an honest experience of being a parent. It's not fair, but it's intense and real, and a burden worth reckoning with. The best antidote we know of is self-compassion. This is difficult work to do. It won't happen easily or quickly. But with awareness and practice, you can get some space between you and shame and start to heal it with acts of kindness toward yourself.

What Causes Shame—and What Shame Causes You to Do

Any number of pathways can lead to feelings of shame. One of the most common is guilt about things that you've said out of anger or confusion (for example, "You're just a drug addict" or "You're a disgrace to this family"). Another way is through misgivings about how you handled things in the past (*I wasn't around enough, I was too hard on him, I didn't know he was depressed*; a time you resorted to violence) or decisions you made along the way (such as letting drug use go unaddressed early on, or sending your loved one away to treatments that ended up being traumatizing). Shame can also come from the stigma associated with substance problems in our culture.

However it arises, harboring shame can push you to isolate or withdraw from others, to make up for errors by trying to be perfect, or to reassign blame to the people around you. Importantly, it doesn't help us reflect, regret, and amend the ways we've come up short or hurt people. Shame is not constructive, and it doesn't help us change.

Isolating. At its core, shame is self-judgment, and it's often accompanied by fear that others are judging you just as harshly. This thinking can sound something like, *If they only knew (fill in the blank), then they wouldn't want to be around me.* It's a particularly destructive aspect of shame, as it causes you to pull away from the support of others. You may find yourself believing that everyone else has their life in order and that you're the only one who's in "this kind of mess." The shame you feel about your own situation may cause you to keep the problem to yourself and suffer alone. Where the shared human experience of struggle or disappointment could connect you to other people who are going through something similar, shame pushes you to keep failings and setbacks to yourself.

As we've discussed in this chapter, it's an act of self-compassion to feel this connection to others and reach out of isolation. The first step might just be to have some compassion for yourself as you're suffering the pain and loneliness of shame. Then, maybe let yourself feel a sense of connection with all your fellow human beings who have also felt lonely and ashamed.

Seeking perfection. Another common reaction to shame is to dedicate an enormous amount of time and energy trying to accomplish the impossible: to avoid the future experience of shame by striving for perfection. Truthfully, everyone has moments they regret—sometimes deeply—and everyone feels disappointed in themselves now and then. Shame makes you think that no one else has "screwed up" as much as you have and that you need to "make sure this never happens again." Perfection-seeking, however, is the opposite of building the resilience you need most in this struggle. The more we strive for perfection and fail to obtain it, the more we may use this as proof that there's something wrong with us.

Externalizing blame. People also respond to shame by turning it on others, convincing themselves that it's the people around them who are at fault. Although this distracts from distress in the short term, self-doubt and self-criticism lurk in the background, only to seep back in later. In addition, this reaction holds you back from taking a closer look at your own behaviors that may be worth changing or modifying. "Failing" and being open to examining your mistakes allows you to learn, grow, and improve. When shame directs your focus to the faults of others, you miss out on that opportunity to grow.

Treating Shame with Self-Compassion

In the end, the answer to shame is self-compassion. Noticing when shame-based thoughts arise (a good example of self-awareness) and working to reframe them in a kinder, more self-accepting way is a powerful step toward relief from the toxic effects of shame.

Let's consider some of the shaming thoughts you most often have—and how you can explore what they might signal, namely regrets you have, without allowing them to reduce your sense of your own worth.

Consider the following examples of shaming thoughts versus reflective or regretful ones.

Shaming Thoughts	Reflecting/Regretful Thoughts
A good parent should have known about ___________ earlier on. (perfectionism)	*I'm so sad I didn't know about ___________ earlier on.*
Maybe I'll skip going out with our friends. It's so humiliating to deal with their questions. (isolating)	*It's painful to answer questions about our daughter.*
My partner's anger is totally unacceptable. (shame turned to blame)	*I wish my partner were able to be less angry.*

You'll see there's a difference between the thoughts on the left, which reflect shame about your or others' personal defects or failures, and the thoughts on the right, which reflect on what's happened in the past in a way that helps you consider how you could react or behave differently in the future.

Next, write several shaming thoughts you've had recently related to interactions, feelings, or events around your loved one's substance use. Then, try to rephrase those thoughts so that they express regret while still being compassionate and not shaming yourself or anyone else.

Shaming Thoughts	Reflecting/Regretful Thoughts

When you're done, consider what it felt like to make the shift in each of your shaming thoughts to more regretful, reflective ones. Was it difficult to do? And—does it make it easier to imagine more self-compassionate, productive, fruitful things you could do the next time you're in a situation that tends to provoke thoughts of shame in yourself and others?

While it can be painful, being aware of the shame you might be feeling can help set you and your loved one on a different course. Again, there's a willingness to this: picking up the whole coin, making the decision to allow for the painful experiences on one side because you value the connection, caring, and compassion that are on the other. In attempting to discard feelings of regret or shame by isolating, seeking perfection, or blaming others, you throw out the possibility for connection, caring, and compassion as well.

Experiencing the emotional part of being human, such as the sadness of loss and the regrets of damage done and opportunities missed, strengthens your connection to other people. You can apologize if you need to. You can ask for support from others who care about you or have gone through similar circumstances. You can unload some of the baggage and move forward. If instead you stay stuck in the shame, dwelling on your "badness" or your family's "defects," shame will likely lead you away from other people and into hiding.

Exercise: Taking a Step Out of Shame and Isolation

These acts may seem small, but they can have deep and rippling effects, especially when you make them—even just one!—a regular part of your life.

- Cook your favorite meal
- Go out to eat somewhere you like
- Let yourself space out and just watch TV
- Meditate or do some other calming activity
- Listen to a podcast
- Read a favorite book or poem
- Write yourself a nice note you can read when you're feeling down
- Learn a new skill
- Take a trip somewhere
- Pray or visit a place of worship that soothes you
- Get some exercise
- Volunteer somewhere new, or just do something to help someone out—giving to others can be a powerful way to help yourself

Write down some additional ideas of your own here:

____

____

____

____

____

____

Exercise: Making a Plan for Self-Compassion

Suffocating from worry, fear, anger, resentment, stress, or shame will not help you help someone else. You need to feel good yourself to be the best possible support for your loved one. We recommend that you spend time each week doing something that makes you feel connected to what's important to you. This could be anything that helps you feel relaxed, valued, competent, soothed—something you want to do as opposed to something you think you should do.

How will you contribute to your own self-care this week? Consider your health (nutrition, sleep, exercise) as well as what nourishes you intellectually, emotionally, and spiritually.

Identify areas of your life that could use a bit of attention, where a change would help you feel less stressed or improve your quality of life. The following questions may help get you started.

1. When was the last time you put any of your interests first? When was the last time you learned something new? The last time you had a discussion about something other than your loved one?

   ____

   ____

   ____

   ____

2. How stressed or anxious do you feel during the day (nervousness, tightness in chest, stomachaches)? How tired do you feel? What do you notice when you lie down to go to sleep (racing thoughts, nervousness, your mind chattering about all the things that are going on for you)? How do these thoughts, feelings, and bodily sensations affect how you're sleeping? Exercising? Eating? Are you ignoring medical issues of your own? When was the last time you had a medical checkup?

____

____

____

____

3. Have you been more reactive lately—short fuse, quick to cry, etc.? Do find yourself feeling numb, closed off, angry? Are you doing or saying things that don't align with who you want to be? When have you said to yourself, "Good job"? Do you have someone that you can share your true feelings with?

____

____

____

____

Pick an area (from above) and brainstorm possible solutions. What would you like to accomplish and why would it help you build the resilience you need to help your loved one?

What I Would Like To Accomplish	Why It Would Help Me
I would like to sleep through the night.	It would help me feel less irritable in the morning, when we often fight.
I would like to find the time to read a good book.	It would help me take a break and feel less resentful about spending all my time worrying about my loved one.

What I Would Like To Accomplish	Why It Would Help Me

Select two solutions and convert them into doable goals. Try to keep them simple, positive, specific and measurable, achievable, within your control, and involving skills that you already have or are learning. Set two self-care goals for the coming week. We recommend at least one of them be something that is entirely enjoyable to you.

1. To improve my self-care, this week I will:

   ____

   ____

   (Examples: I will go for a run two times this week to blow off steam and feel more tired when I go to bed. This will help me sleep better. I will try not to beat myself up or second-guess myself.)

2. To increase joy in my life, I will:

   ____

   ____

   (Example: I will go to the bookstore on my way home from work and buy a new book. Then I will stop doing chores at 10 p.m. and get lost in my book.)

Identify obstacles that could interfere with your goals for the week.

Obstacles to Achieving My Goal	Coping Strategies for Dealing with the Obstacles
It's hard to find time to go for a run.	Plan out the week and schedule time for runs around other activities. Commit to it like an appointment.
I'm too worried to sit and read. I get distracted.	Take deep breaths and give myself permission to start small. If I can read for fifteen minutes, that's better than no break at all.

Putting It All Together

Self-compassion is an invaluable practice when you're helping a loved one who's suffering from substance use. It sustains you through times of struggle, models behavior you'd like your loved one to adopt, lets you reach out to others for support, and helps you overcome shame.

No matter how you structure your practice of self-compassion, we encourage you to continue using the helping-on-the-inside tools provided in this chapter to bolster yourself as you move to the next part of the book: the action you'll take on the outside to invite your loved one to change, now that you have the understanding and awareness you need.

PART THREE

Helping with Action

So far, we've covered two important ways of helping someone (and yourself) by making changes within yourself. Helping with Understanding shifts your perspective on the problem you face and increases your empathy for your loved one to create the conditions for change. Helping with Awareness connects you to your emotions, thoughts, and values so that you can pursue what matters most, quiet the judgmental self-talk in your head, and replenish your resilience for helping over the long run. This third part, Helping with Action, is about what you can do out in the world. In it, we offer practical tools to improve your interactions with your loved one, concentrating on the aspects of your interactions that are within your control: how you talk and how you act. How you talk and act will have a huge impact on your loved one's willingness to consider change and how they go about doing it. Your words and behavior can be powerful motivators for your loved one and can serve as a model for the behaviors you hope to see more of.

Remember, with ITC we're inviting change, not forcing it. Trying to force someone to behave differently is, at best, a short-term solution, if it's a solution at all. Too often, it can backfire or make things worse. We invite you to pause and consider, *As I try to help, what impact do I want to have on my loved one's choices and on our relationship?*

We also encourage you to focus on small, achievable changes in your relationship with your loved one and your loved one's treatment, rather than push for big, dramatic ones. It's tempting to swing the sledgehammer out of desperation for *big* change *now*, but small changes are more likely to produce the long-term results that we're hoping for: greater connection with our loved ones, greater ownership on their part of their change process, and knowing that we acted in line with our deepest values. Instead of a sledgehammer, think of water running over land on its way to the ocean. A single drop of water doesn't have much effect, but—as anyone who has visited the Grand Canyon can tell you—like streams and rivers, many small changes over time have the power to reshape whole landscapes and lives.

The action we invite you to take in this part of the book will help you invite your loved one to practice new, positive behaviors, such as taking better care of themselves, pursuing new interests, reducing (or eliminating) substance use, and having better interactions with you. We offer evidence-based communication strategies to help you decrease conflict and promote open dialogue about change, and behavior strategies proven to help you increase your loved one's motivation to engage in healthy habits and decrease their harmful behaviors. You'll learn how to respect your own limits and to allow natural consequences to play a role in the learning process.

Finally, since no one enters this world as an expert in helping, we will remind you, again, of the need to practice, practice, practice. Learning to use these communication and behavior tools is no exception.

Words from a fellow traveler: *We used to panic and give her money when she seemed desperate, even though we knew she probably spent it on drugs. We are taking better care of ourselves now, so we panic less, and can plan better for how to handle those moments. We give her a little extra money when she has made it to work every day for a week. If she runs out because she's been using, we have told her in advance we won't give her any to get by and we support each other to hold this line when she's desperate. It's hard, but she is asking us for money less and less and we feel good giving her a little extra when she has a good week.*

CHAPTER 7

Good Communication Turns Red Lights Green

Communication that is collaborative instead of controlling, confrontational, one-sided, or dismissive of your loved one's perspective decreases defensiveness and invites conversations that support change.

All we ever do is shout at each other or shut each other down.

They just need to hit rock bottom—conversations don't really help.

I'm just talking to the "addict brain."

I say the same things over and over, but he doesn't listen.

She doesn't care what I say.

You've probably already tried to talk to your loved one about changing their behavior, and it's likely that despite your good intentions, the conversations have gone off course and become unproductive or downright destructive. You might despair that there's anything you can say.

But this kind of thinking isn't helpful, and it doesn't have to be true.

Communication often takes a serious hit during times of stress and heightened emotion—and when someone you love is struggling with a scary behavior like misusing substances, discussions tend to focus on the latest disappointment or the last time they used. When they turn into arguments or shouting matches, conversations become things to avoid, as everyone involved feels unheard and unsupported. Ultimately, communication between you and the person you care about can come to a total halt. But there are tools you can use to listen to, empathize with, and validate your loved one, and there are ways to communicate to them the changes in their behavior you want to see. ITC allows you to have even the hardest conversations with patience, compassion for yourself and your loved one, and the willingness to do whatever can be done, right here and right now, to help your loved one along the path to change.

A New Perspective on Communication

Good communication matters deeply. Words—how they're spoken and received—matter. They are how we understand each other, care for each other, agree or disagree with each other, support each other, and stay connected to each other. The words we use can create safety, trust, meaning, and space for change, or they can destroy any hope of connection.

When it's done well—with love, respect, and empathy—communication results in a deeper connection between you and your loved one and allows everyone to feel heard and respected, which, in turn, improves collaboration. A collaborative approach to conversation can help change the tone in your home from closed to open, and in the process reduce conflict. Creating a collaborative environment will also give your loved one space to find their own reasons to alter their behavior—a crucial component of sustained change. In other words, effective, collaborative, and respectful communication shifts ambivalence and tips the motivational seesaw toward change.

Practicing the communication strategies in this chapter may be the most powerful thing you can do to improve your situation and help your loved one.

Watching for Red and Green Lights

Before moving on to specific tools for improving communication, we'll start with a very basic idea: if you want to hear and be heard, you need to pay attention to the signals your conversation partner is giving you. To expand on this analogy, paying attention to traffic lights while driving is necessary to navigate the roads safely; similarly, paying attention to cues from the other person, both before and during a conversation, makes productive communication much more likely.

When heeded, **conversational red lights** can warn you of impending danger and help you prevent a crash. These signals include body language—such as lack of eye contact, crossed arms, or back turned to you—as well as behaviors—like walking away or slamming doors. They also include tone of voice and words like "not now" that indicate less readiness to engage, talk, or listen.

If red lights are present, the conversation is probably not having the effect you want—in fact, it's at risk of crashing. Pushing past these red lights to get something off your chest likely won't result in anyone being heard, but it will cause emotions to rise or your loved one to shut down. It can be tempting to gun it through the red lights by talking over them or speaking louder, but you probably know from experience that when you fight, you say things you regret and feel worse instead of better. What's more, arguments give your loved one the opportunity to practice talking (or yelling) about all the reasons why they shouldn't change and why you're the problem. Then you're not just standing still; you've gone backward.

The tools and strategies in this chapter will help you turn the red lights green, or at least yellow, but to do this successfully, you first have to pay attention to your loved one's signals. And this involves willingness.

When we're frustrated and upset by someone's behavior and we don't want to feel that way anymore, it can seem like shouting can make the feeling go away. And sometimes it does! When you speed past the red light, however, you're moving away from things you value, such as connection and being heard. Moving toward the things you value takes willingness to be with the pain and frustration long enough to heed your loved one's signals. If you're willing to allow your frustration to be there, without requiring that it be immediately resolved, you open the possibility of having connected conversations, or at least limiting the destructive ones. Taking several breaths and approaching the conversation later can feel frustrating, but it may be the path to what you really want.

Take a moment to think about signals you get from your loved one. And remember, those light signals don't have to be spoken; they can be body language, situations that you know will be difficult, and so on. We've started you off with a few examples.

Some of my loved one's red lights that I've noticed:

- Saying "I don't want to talk right now"
- Rushing past me as I was hoping to ask a question
- Using shorter and shorter sentences in the middle of our discussion
- ______________________________
- ______________________________
- ______________________________

Some of my loved one's green lights that I've noticed:

- Lingering at the table after dinner
- Saying "Can we talk?"
- Asking me how I'm doing
- Offering to help
- ______________________________
- ______________________________
- ______________________________

Disregarding the lights you see (or can reasonably expect to see) can lead you into conversations that take you further from the change you hope to see. Paying attention to the signals can help you stay on course and keep the conversation moving toward your goals.

In the rest of this chapter, we'll describe specific tools to improve communication and collaboration, and strategies for using them. In addition to improving collaboration, these practices will help you use conversations to make requests, reinforce positive behaviors, and set limits.

First, though, let's consider the different conversational traps we can sometimes fall into with our loved ones.

Conversational Traps

When communication is not going well, and your loved one is being secretive, angry, argumentative, or dishonest, you may find yourself resorting to certain old scripts in an attempt to break through. However, these old ways of communicating may be full of **conversational traps**—automatic, often emotional responses to not feeling like you're heard or on the same team. We all fall into these traps at times, especially when discussing emotionally charged topics. Unfortunately, they tend to push communication into a worse place rather than a better one, leading to more frustration and misunderstanding.

Here are some common traps to be aware of as you begin to implement different communication strategies with your loved one on the path to change.

- **The Information Trap:** "If only he knew the facts, he'd see things differently!" Information can be helpful, especially when it fills a gap in someone's knowledge. It's not so helpful, however, to tell your loved one something that they already know or to repeat the same information over and over.
- **The Lecture Trap:** This is the heavier-handed cousin of the information trap. It says, "I know what's best for you" and "You need to hear this!" A sign you've entered this trap is when you find yourself talking at someone rather than with them, or notice you've been speaking for more than a few minutes without hearing from the other person.

- **The Label Trap:** In general, labels are not helpful; they often get in the way of change, causing defensiveness and a tendency to fight about the label itself. ("You're an addict." "No, I'm not.") This pulls the focus away from what you really want to talk about, like your concerns about your loved one's safety.
- **The Blame Trap:** When we're scared or upset, it's easy to get stuck trying to assign blame for the problem. This shuts down conversation and risks backing your loved one into a corner, where they'll usually fight you and lose motivation to change. This includes blaming the substance use for all the problems, as in "If you would only stop drinking, everything would be fine!"
- **The Taking-Sides Trap:** If you take only one side in a discussion ("Drug use is horrible!" or "That boyfriend of yours is bad news"), you set your loved one up to take the other, and they may end up defending behaviors that they actually aren't so sure about.
- **The Question-and-Answer Trap:** Asking your loved one closed questions (described below) can make a conversation feel like an interview—or worse, an interrogation. ("Did you get high last night? Where were you? Who were you with? Did you forget your phone? Did you do your homework?") These types of conversations are one-sided and often at risk of being shut down.

It's easy to veer into these conversational traps when feeling stressed, angry, frightened, or frustrated by the red lights someone is putting up. They're understandable responses to pain or discomfort, and the desire to get past those feelings by taking charge instead of collaborating can be pretty strong. When we do this, however, we move away from what we value and strive for, such as being heard, communicating effectively, staying connected to the other person, and influencing positive change. Being aware of the traps can help you notice when you fall into them, so you can adjust course, or plan ahead and avoid getting caught.

Communication Strategies

Now, let's look at the specific tools you can use to move toward what really matters to you. We're going to offer two overall communication strategies—LOVE and SURF. Both of these strategies have multiple parts, many of which have their own exercises, so you may want to bookmark this page so you can flip back and forth as you read. To help you remember them (or refresh your memory), here's a quick outline of what they stand for:

Communication Strategy #1: LOVE—How to Deepen Connection

- **L**istening
- **O**ffering Information
- **V**alidating
- **E**mpathizing

The "Listen" part of LOVE involves two other skills: simply listening (or paying attention to what the other person is saying) and skillful listening (or listening with the goal of considerate responding). Skillful listening uses another set of tools, known as OARS:

- Asking **O**pen-Ended Questions
- **A**ffirming
- **R**eflecting Back
- **S**ummarizing

Communication Strategy #2: SURF—How to Make Requests

- Be **S**pecific
- Offer an **U**nderstanding Statement
- Take Partial **R**esponsibility
- Label Your **F**eelings

This chapter provides a lot of detail and several exercises on effective communication skills. Take your time with it. The skills may seem complicated at first, but as you dive in and practice them, they'll make more sense.

Communication Strategy #1: Communicating with LOVE

You've probably heard it said that love is not just something we're in, but something we do. For our purposes, the acronym LOVE captures four important things you can do to communicate caring and invite change:

Listening

Offering Information

Validating

Empathizing

LOVE isn't so much a step-by-step process as a menu of options for helpful communication with your loved one (or anyone). Having the flexibility of these options can help you turn red lights green and avoid falling into conversational traps.

*Listening (**L**OVE)*

We start with listening and spend some time on it for a reason: being heard and understood is a powerful and comforting experience and leads to more and more constructive interactions. Think about past conversations in which you had space to talk, were not talked over, and knew that the other person was listening. Perhaps you thought to yourself, *This person really gets me*, or just had the feeling that they cared.

While listening seems easy enough, we're all familiar with the experience of speaking with someone who doesn't seem to be taking in what we're saying. Too often, conversations about substance use end with both people feeling as if the other wasn't listening.

What commonly gets in the way of just listening? Maybe you're distracted by the chatter in your head or are formulating your response before the other person is even done talking. Maybe you get caught up in difficult emotions or preoccupied by the million other things you need to be doing. Whatever the cause, it happens all the time! And not listening well can prevent you from being an effective helper.

There are two types of helpful listening: simply listening and skillful listening. Each can have a profound impact on both you and your loved one. Either kind of listening gives the other person room to say what they're thinking, which gives you more information to work with as you try to help them. It can help them feel safer and increase connection, compassion, and hope—all of which can open them to change. Your willingness to listen can also help reduce the shame and stigma associated with their substance problems and allow them to be honest about struggling.

Importantly, you don't have to have the answers in the moment or control over what comes next; just the act of listening will go a long way.

Listening 1.0: Simply Listening

The simplest way to turn red lights green—and a good beginning to any conversation, before you respond at all—is **simply listening.** This type of listening requires you to do just that: just pay attention to what the other person is saying and try to understand them. Simply listening can involve gestures to indicate you're listening, like making eye contact, nodding your head, smiling, or making other facial expressions, but it requires that you do not interrupt, talk over, or comment in a way that stops the other person from talking. It also means letting go of the common habit of planning your response while the other person is still speaking. Note that simply listening is simple in theory, but that doesn't mean it will feel easy in practice.

Exercise: Simply Listening

We invite you to set the goal to simply listen during a conversation today. It can be with your loved one or someone else, such as a coworker, family member, or friend. Let the person know you want to practice just listening and ask them to tell you about their day. In the beginning, start small—try to simply listen for two to three minutes. As you listen, notice what the experience is like for you. Afterward, think about the following questions:

What did you notice when you were listening?

____

____

____

What feelings or physical sensations did you notice?

____

____

What thoughts did you have?

____

____

____

____

How strong was the pull to talk or comment or plan your response?

____

____

Did you experience anything positive while simply listening?

____

____

____

If you have a willing partner, you could also try reversing the roles so that you can experience being simply listened *to* as well. It can be quite powerful to realize the impact of providing another person with your undivided attention, free from any agenda.

Now, let's look at how we can go beyond simple listening by learning how best to respond to the people we listen to.

Listening 2.0: Skillful Listening

Skillful listening builds on simply listening with considerate, empathetic responding. It's based on a powerful therapeutic approach called motivational interviewing (Miller and Rollnick 2013) that emphasizes four tools for increasing open communication: Asking Open-ended questions, Affirming, Reflecting back, and Summarizing, which you can remember with the acronym OARS. Skillful listening increases the likelihood that the person you're talking to will feel heard and encouraged to talk. This often inspires them to listen to you in return, and voilà—green lights all around.

We'll introduce the tools here and offer you some exercises to practice with them.

Asking Open-ended questions (OARS—Skillful Listening). Questions that can be answered with a single word, like "yes" or "no," are closed questions. They usually don't take conversations very far, and they can push a conversation into the question-and-answer trap. **Open-ended questions**, on the other hand—questions that begin with words or phrases such as "how," "what," or "please tell me more about"—can't be answered with one word. They invite description, giving you, the listener, more to hear and learn from. They also set a collaborative tone, as they communicate interest in the other person's view.

Although the question "why" seems to be an open-ended question, be wary of starting this way. Often questions that start with "why" feel like an interrogation. "Why are you still using?" feels different to hear than "What about using is important to you?"

Here are some examples of closed and open-ended questions.

Closed Question	Open-Ended Question
"Are you mad that your friend called me to say she was worried?"	"How are you reacting to your friend calling me to say she's worried?"
"Why do you think you shouldn't have a curfew?"	"What about this curfew do you think is unfair?"
"Did work go alright today?"	"What went on at work today?"
"Don't you think you should ____________?"	"What are your thoughts about ________?"

In the space below, you'll find some examples of closed questions. Try to turn each one into an open-ended question. Then, think about some of the closed questions you've asked your loved one in the past, and try to make those open-ended ones too.

Closed Question	Open-Ended Question
"Couldn't you have just said no?"	
"Are you having a hard time stopping smoking?"	
"Are you ever going to take this seriously?"	

Affirming (OARS—Skillful Listening). Conversations can easily become all about what's wrong, overshadowing what is going well. **Affirmations**—comments that explicitly acknowledge the positive—can rebalance the conversation and increase your chances of seeing green lights. They also reduce defensiveness, which helps when you do get around to discussing tougher issues. They can build your loved one's self-esteem (often in short supply) and reinforce positive behaviors.

Note that unlike general cheerleading ("You're doing great"), affirmations applaud specific actions or situations ("I appreciate your thoughtfulness with my mother today"). For example, you can:

- Acknowledge effort ("You're really showing commitment to getting home on time.")
- State your appreciation ("I appreciate your openness and honesty today.")
- Catch them doing something nice ("Thanks for helping me out in the kitchen.")
- Give a compliment ("I like the way you said that. You really have a way with people.")
- Express hope, caring, or support ("I hope this weekend goes well for you!")

Highlighting your loved one's strengths and recognizing their positive behaviors lowers defensiveness and increases motivation. And remember, an affirmation can be as simple as "Thank you." Let's practice offering affirmations now.

In this exercise, note some ways that your loved one has tried to explain their behavior in the past, then imagine affirming responses you could use to recognize the behavior that you want them to continue.

Their Explanation (examples)	Your Affirmation (examples)
"I tried not to use, but it didn't work out last night."	"You took a stab at doing something difficult."
"I know I didn't tell you until you asked me about it."	"I appreciate your talking honestly to me about this now."
"I *did* at least try not to start drinking until later in the party…"	"It took some courage to try something different last night."
"I always seem to run into the wrong people when I go out."	
"I didn't go with my friends to the park yesterday, but it was freaking hard saying no and it made me really resentful."	

Their Explanation (examples)	Your Affirmation (examples)
"I don't know how long I can keep up this sober thing."	

Now, let's try something a bit more challenging. Think about the strong emotions you sometimes struggle with, or the difficult, even terrifying experiences your loved one's choices may have put you through. It can be very hard to figure out how to use affirmations in such moments. And it makes sense that once you've been through them, you may be more sensitive to problems or warning signs than anything that is going well. We're all prone to be attuned to danger; it's our mind's way of protecting us.

But in these moments, too, you can look for aspects of your loved one's situation or behavior to affirm. And affirmation can help make it easier to find your way through the tough things you and your loved one are facing.

Consider the scenario below.

I'm sick of this, everything just keeps getting messed up. I tried to talk with my boss, but she did not have time for me, and now it's my fault I didn't get the project in by the deadline! And no one seems to care that I'm working on five other things. What's the point in even trying? Sometimes I'll decide to just leave work early and go for a drink, but then everyone I hang out with talks about how great they're doing. It's so messed up, because if I don't get this promotion, I won't be able to afford my kid's tuition, and that's the only thing that keeps me going these days.

What are two statements you could offer that would highlight strengths or positive steps? Keep in mind that this exercise is asking you to pay attention to things to affirm. Remember to be specific.

1. ____

____

2. ____

____

Here's another example of a statement for which it might be difficult to find things to affirm:

> *I don't have a problem with drinking or pot. I know I have to stay away from the pills, but I know what I can handle and what I can't. I don't agree with the people in the meetings. They don't know me. I know I don't want to ruin my life and I need to stay focused on finding a job and staying away from what was my real problem—heroin.*

What are two statements you could offer that would highlight strengths/affirm positive steps? Again, be specific.

1. ____

____

2. ____

____

Now, think back to the last tough situation you faced with your loved one—maybe one in which you blew a red light, reacting impulsively or harshly in ways that made the situation harder to deal with. Are there affirmations you could have made instead—ones that might've made the situation easier for you and your loved one to get through (without excusing their behavior or ignoring the aspects of the situation that may have hurt you or others)?

____

____

____

____

Reflecting Back (OARS—Skillfull Listening). Reflections (also called active listening) involve restating some or all of what you think your conversation partner has said. Reflections communicate to the other person that you're actually listening and trying to understand what they're saying. Whether you get it right or wrong, reflections are win-win: if you correctly state what they said, they feel heard; if you get it wrong, they have the chance to correct you and make sure that you're both on the same page. Reflecting is not necessarily agreeing, but it shows a willingness to hear the other person's perspective, instead of immediately countering their ideas or statements. Reflective listening helps a discussion move forward even after you've hit a red light.

In motivational interviewing, there are several different kinds of reflections, but we're going to focus on two: simple reflections and double-sided ones.

1. Simple reflections capture what a person has said and give it back to them pretty much as spoken. They can be word for word or paraphrased.

   Speaker: "I really didn't like the movie."

   Listener: "There was something about that movie you really didn't like!" (simple reflection)

   or

   Speaker: "I get worked up when I have to speak to him."

   Listener: "Talking with him pushes your buttons." (simple reflection)

2. Double-sided reflections help you approach mixed feelings or ambivalence expressed by the other person. When you hear someone waffling or showing uncertainty, it can be tempting to take one side of the debate. For example, it's challenging to hear about your loved one's reasons for using, and you may find yourself pointing out all the reasons for not using ("Your drinking is ruining our relationship"—note the blame trap). In return, you may have found that this leads to their defending their behavior or telling you why they can't change ("My drinking is not the problem, you are"—blaming back at you).

   Double-sided reflections avoid the conversational trap of taking sides because they allow both sides of the discussion to be heard. They give the other person room to voice competing thoughts without putting you in a position where they want to push back at you.

   Speaker: "I really want to get in shape, but with work it's impossible to exercise."

   Listener: "Seems like it's important to you to get more exercise, and finding the time is challenging." (double-sided reflection)

   or

   Speaker: "I know drinking is bad for me, but I just have so much stress and it helps at the end of the day."

   Listener: "Drinking helps you relax, and you're concerned that it may affect your health." (double-sided reflection)

   Note: Notice the use of the word "and" in the double-sided reflections. The word "but" can work against you by discounting everything that comes before it. The word "and" allows both voices to be present without taking a side.

To practice the skill of reflecting back, think of some comments or feelings that your loved one has shared with you and recall how you responded in the moment. Then, try to adjust your response to make it reflective. Notice the impulse to correct your loved one (which will usually be met with a justification of their rightness) or to offer a solution (which can often be met with an objection)—both of which are conversational traps. If you can create space for the other person to express their version of events, you'll improve the odds that, eventually, they'll also be able to hear another perspective.

Remember: Give yourself time with these new practices. Taking a bit of time each day, instead of feeling you need to know it all at once, is a helpful way to approach this.

Loved One's Statement	Non-reflective Response (less effective)	Reflective Response (more effective)
"You never listen to me."	"That's not true, I…"	"You feel you're not being heard."
"I don't want to stop drinking."	"Don't you see that you have a problem?!"	"Alcohol is really important to you."
"I didn't use last night."	"Yeah, but it's only one night."	"Not using was a priority for you last night and you were successful."
"You're making a big deal out of nothing, I don't have a problem."		
"I don't need your help."		

Summarizing (OARS—Skillfull Listening). When you ask open-ended questions, provide affirmations, and reflect back what someone is saying, you may find yourself in a long and productive conversation! Summarizing at the end communicates that you were listening and helps underline the important things that were said. It also allows the other person to organize their thoughts and can lead them to connect the dots around certain behaviors. Summaries can even guide the conversation toward a next step, without forcing an agenda. Like reflections, summaries should come with permission for the other person to disagree with or correct the record as you recount it. Summary statements are really just a collection of reflections, so they should be as accurate as possible, without adding in what you wished your loved one had said.

Look at all the tools you already have at your disposal just from Listening! Now that we've covered how to Listen with LOVE, let's move on to the next step in the communication with LOVE strategy: Offering Information.

Offering Information (LOVE)

The next part of communicating with LOVE will help you offer feedback or information. Have you ever wanted to say to your partner, "You know, heavy drinking is probably contributing to your depression," but didn't because you dreaded the response? Have you ever been tempted to say to your daughter, "The evidence is in—cigarette smoking kills. Why don't you just quit already?" but stopped yourself because she's shut down that conversation a million times? Way too often, we offer feedback or observations that we think will be helpful, only to have the conversation go off track—or worse, end up in a conversational trap (the information or lecture trap) that leads to hurt feelings and disappointment.

Don't give up! There are ways to improve your ability to engage your loved one in a conversation about your concerns. They might not want to hear what you have to say—for a variety of reasons that may include shame, guilt, ambivalence, or simple disagreement—but you can still learn to offer information in a helpful way, which matters a lot: you have stuff to say!

The **information sandwich** is a three-step technique for making the information that you want to share (the contents of the "sandwich") palatable to your loved one. By sandwiching—asking permission, providing information, and checking back—you help your loved one receive the feedback, take it in, and consider using it. You may find that this skill comes in handy with many other people in your life, too.

Asking permission. This is the conversational equivalent of knocking before you enter a room, and it has several benefits. When you ask for permission to share information, the other person has an opportunity to invite you in, which can have a profound impact on their motivation. Consider how you feel when someone shows up at your house unexpectedly. Do you feel annoyed that you're being interrupted? Stressed that your house is a mess? You likely feel different than you would if you'd invited them over for a visit and were prepared and comfortable in your environment. By asking permission, you give someone the chance to be open and ready for the conversation you hope to have.

Here are a few ways to ask permission before sharing information:

- "Would it be helpful for you to hear about…?"
- "Could I offer a thought?"
- "Can I ask a question?"
- "I have a couple of ideas, but did you want to say your ideas first?"
- "Would it be alright if I expressed one concern I have about this plan?"

People are more likely to hear, appreciate, and use information that is offered rather than forced. Asking permission is one way to make sure the light is green before you proceed with the content of your discussion. In fact, it can increase the frequency of green lights, as it builds the other person's sense of safety and control and honors their independence by providing a choice. When they feel as if they're a participant in the conversation, not just a passive or reluctant recipient of your words, it sets the stage for you to talk with them instead of at them, increasing the likelihood that they'll hear what you say next.

One last point: Truly asking permission means leaving room for them to say "No, I'd rather not hear this right now." While this response may be painful or maddening to hear, it's better to know this than to ignore the red light and launch into another conversation that goes nowhere fast. In these moments, you can try asking if there's a better time to have the conversation, or just step away and try again later.

Providing information. Once permission is granted, you can share the information or feedback you have to offer. This information can be anything: schedules for the day, gossip you heard, deadlines approaching, medical information, and so on.

It may help to provide options, when it makes sense, if you're suggesting a particular course of action. Offering more than one good option puts the other person in the position to weigh the pros and cons of each rather than simply saying "no."

Finally, remember to only do what you have received consent to do in the asking permission stage, as this builds trust over time. If you said the conversation will only take two minutes, then keep it short.

Checking back or clarifying. The last layer of the sandwich helps the other person process the information and remain open to the discussion. Essentially, you want to know how the information was received. Did they understand the feedback, or did they get too mad, hurt, or sad to take in what you said? Or perhaps they were just spaced out. Here are some examples of checking back:

- "Does that make sense to you?"
- "I just wanted to check back about..."
- "I'm not sure I said that very clearly..."

As in the first step, it's critical here to allow disagreement. As much as possible, leave room for the other person to not accept or agree with the information. And as in every step of communication—and every step of the Invitation to Change—tone is important. Remember, kindness is the glue that holds it all together. Science plus kindness equals change.

Ultimately, the information you wish to share will only be helpful if it's heard. Asking permission, providing options, and checking back will make the difference in whether that information is taken in. It's still possible that your loved one will disagree with you. It may be difficult, but do your best to let it happen when it does without pushing back aggressively. Remember, collaborators don't tell each other what to do; they resolve issues together. By allowing for disagreement, you give the conversation a chance to move forward instead of coming to a screeching halt or head-on collision. And by allowing your loved one the freedom to agree or disagree, you'll encounter less defensiveness—in other words, more green lights.

Let's practice the sandwich technique now.

Exercise: Practicing the Sandwich

Think of a circumstance in which you have information or feedback to give—to your loved one or to another person in your life—about substance use or anything else. This exercise outlines how to build an information sandwich around what you want to offer.

1. Start with the middle layer (the information you hope to share) and consider how the other person might react. Write down the information or feedback you'd like to give to this person.

I'd like to let ___________ [person's name] know that

____

____

2. Next, plan how you'll ask for permission first and how you'll check back after, considering how the delivery might affect the other person's reaction to the information. What kind of reaction do you imagine? What red or green lights might appear?

   ____

   ____

3. Now, put the content from step 1 in a sandwich:

   How will you ask for permission to give them this information?

   ____

   ____

   How will you check back?

   ____

   ____

4. Consider how this interaction might go differently (versus what you anticipated) after using the information sandwich.

   ____

   ____

Remember, you can practice any new skill in lower-risk situations and with other people before trying it with your loved one under more challenging circumstances.

The last two actions in our LOVE acronym (Validating and Empathizing) involve acknowledging that the other person's experience—their thoughts, feelings, motivations, and perspectives—are real to them (validating) and imagining what it's like to walk in their shoes (empathizing). As with reflections, you can validate and empathize without agreeing with or endorsing someone's behavior.

Validating (LOVE)

One of the things we want most is to be understood. That is, having others see how our thoughts, feelings, and responses make sense to us given the situation (remember the discussion, in chapter 2, about behaviors making sense). Yet often people tell us we shouldn't feel a certain way or that our perspective or response to a situation is wrong or not true. These communications send the message that what we feel, think, or do is not allowed, is not worthy, or is not real.

To understand someone else's perspective and responses we must listen and observe carefully, which means eliminating distractions—putting down our phone, shutting off the TV or computer—and giving them our undivided attention; from there, communicating to them that what they say, feel, or do is understandable, given their situation. Validating is the act of recognizing another person's experiences without judgment. It's acknowledging that their feelings are understandable in a given situation, and you're not going to tell them to stop feeling or seeing things that way. While this may sound simple, it's often one of the hardest parts of a relationship.

It also comes with some caveats. Validating does not require you to agree with the other person, feel the same way as they do, or turn a blind eye to their behavior. But by validating what they're experiencing through your words and tone of voice, you can lessen defensiveness and invite further conversation. In return, the other person will be more apt to hear and accept your feelings and perspective, even if they don't agree with you.

A Special Note to Parents: If your loved one is an adolescent or young adult, keep in mind that they may naturally be struggling to define who they are and what they can and cannot do, with particular sensitivity to "who's the boss of them." Young people with substance problems commonly hear that their opinions, feelings, and perspectives are not right or are untrue, making them feel invalidated and not accepted by the people in their lives. When you validate a young person's experience instead of telling them that what they're doing makes no sense, you remove a major barrier from the conversation and are more likely to keep them talking to you—often a difficult feat with teenagers.

Exercise: Practicing Validating

There are many ways to validate someone's experience. Small actions, such as making eye contact and not looking at your phone, can really add up. You can also practice saying things like "I understand that you feel ________________________, and that makes sense to me, because you've said ________________________ in the past."

This sentence shows that you observed and listened, and based on what you know about their experiences, demonstrates that you understand and accept how they feel and how they arrived at that feeling.

You can also validate by connecting the other person's experience back to yourself: "I get it, because if someone had done ________________________ to me, I'd also feel ________________________."

Again, by showing that you listened to the other person and naming how they felt you indicated that you could identify with them.

When you hold back your judgments and opinions, you can learn more about your loved one and create an environment of caring and respect, which will go a long way toward improving the quality of your relationship.

Empathizing (LOVE)

If validating is holding back judgments, then acknowledging and accepting that someone experiences things a certain way—or empathizing—is actively letting them know you're trying to understand their perspective. While it can be hard to put yourself in another person's shoes or feel how someone else is feeling, careful listening and accurate reflection of what they're saying can signal that you "get it." Empathizing is a gracious and caring thing to do, one that comes naturally to some and less so to others, but even showing that we're trying to "get it," even if we don't get it right, can turn red lights green. We know it can be particularly challenging to hear your loved one's perspective when they're doing things that upset you, yet that is where empathic listening is perhaps most powerful for building or maintaining a connection with them and lessening anger and upset as well.

Again, empathizing doesn't necessarily mean agreeing; it's showing the other person you're trying to feel it from their perspective. Empathy can be communicated in reflective statements with very few words: "Wow, that seems really scary," or "That really made you mad," or "You're really proud of how you handled last night." Statements like these reduce shame and help your loved one open up to new ways of thinking about things.

Exercise: Practicing Empathizing

Reflective listening is key to building empathy. We introduced this tool in the listening section above. When you accurately state something you heard during a conversation, you send a signal that you're trying to understand the other person's perspective or dilemma. You also provide the speaker with an opportunity to correct you if what you heard is not what they said or meant, which keeps the discussion collaborative and gets you both on the same page of the conversation.

You can practice validating and empathizing in almost any conversation. Start with easier, less stressful situations, rather than launching into the most important and tension-filled topic.

What Communicating with LOVE Can Look Like

Remember, LOVE is a menu of options for productive conversation. Here are some examples of how the LOVE tools allow for a range of responses and options to use separately or in combination, all in the service of increasing the chances of moving the conversation forward through green lights:

Child/loved one: "I'm going to fail this test either way, since the teacher hates me. Who cares if I study? It makes me want to go smoke instead."

Parent: (reflecting) "You think you're going to fail your test, which makes you not want to study and to smoke instead."

Parent: (validating) "It totally makes sense how it can be hard to stay motivated when you feel so discouraged."

Parent: (affirming) "I really appreciate your letting me know what's going on with you."

Parent: (offering) "Would it be okay for me to offer an idea about this?"

or

Partner/loved one: "I don't have a problem with alcohol—there are worse things out there, and it helps me take the edge off. I wish everyone would just get off my back about this. I'm going to work and I'm taking care of what I need to every day."

Partner: (reflecting, empathizing) "You see your drinking differently than others do."

Partner: (reflecting, empathizing) "Seems like you're feeling a lot of pressure from other people about this."

Partner: (validating) "It makes sense that you feel annoyed if all you're hearing is everyone's concerns all the time."

Partner: (affirming) "I noticed you've been working and doing a lot around the house—I really appreciate that."

Partner: (asking permission to offer information or feedback) "Would it be okay for me to share some of my ideas about this?"

As you consider these examples, take a moment to think about something your loved one recently said that you found difficult to respond to. Maybe the conversation led to a conversational trap that you couldn't quite recover from. Take some time to use the LOVE tools you've just learned to plot out a different, perhaps more effective way you might've responded to the statement or problem.

____

____

____

____

____

____

Communication Strategy #2: SURFing a Request

LOVE tools create the conditions for more open and constructive communication through a stronger connection between speaker and listener. However, no doubt there are times when you'd like to use your words to influence your loved one's behavior. You may be thinking, *I want to have a say in things. How can I put my requests out there? How can I ask for what I want or need?*

Here's where the SURF tools come in. These tools can be applied in a variety of ways, but they're especially helpful when making a request:

S—Be **S**pecific

U—Offer an **U**nderstanding Statement

R—Take Partial **R**esponsibility

F—Label Your **F**eelings

When you use these strategies to make a request, you increase your chances of being heard while simultaneously making the other person feel listened to, optimizing conditions to receive a reasonable response to your request (but no guarantees!).

*Be **S**pecific (**S**URF)*

Most people say more than necessary when they haven't planned a request in advance, especially when they're nervous or angry. If your request is brief and focused on a specific behavior, you can avoid the request's getting lost in the noise. (You don't want to sound like the teacher in *Peanuts*: "Wah wah wah"!) Try to home in on your central request ahead of time and then rehearse what you want to say as concisely as possible. Extra words can drown out your core message. Notice the difference between the following two statements. The first is nonspecific and rambling, and the second is specific and brief:

"During the week, when you have school/work—which is really important—I want you to be more responsible in the morning and help me out by not being late."

versus

"I'd like you to get up when your alarm goes off."

In the first version, the point is less clear. What are they asking of their loved one? To be more responsible? To care more about school/work? To not be late? To help out? The second version offers clear information about what the person wants and what their loved one can do to meet it.

Offer an Understanding Statement (SURF)

Feeling understood vastly increases one's willingness to cooperate. When you use an understanding statement as part of a request, it shows that you realize that the desired outcome might be difficult for your loved one. It also makes your request sound more like a request and less like a demand, which will lower their defensiveness, making them more open to hearing what you have to say.

- Specific: "I'd like you to get up when your alarm goes off."
- Understanding: "I know those early mornings are tough!"

Take Partial Responsibility (SURF)

Sharing in a problem, even a tiny piece of the problem, decreases defensiveness and increases openness. It shows the other person that you're interested in working together, not blaming. This can have an almost magical impact, changing their perception from feeling as though they're being lectured or nagged to feeling that they're being respectfully asked to do something. You might be thinking, *They're the one who needs to change.* But accepting partial responsibility doesn't mean taking blame for a situation that isn't yours to claim. It means claiming the part that you actually and honestly wish you'd done differently. When you're willing to accept responsibility for the parts of the situation you truly have some control over, you communicate that you and your loved one are collaborators in trying to improve the situation.

- Specific: "I'd like you to get up when your alarm goes off."
- Understanding: "I know those early mornings are tough!"
- Responsibility: "And yes, truth be told, I've made mornings more stressful by yelling at you sometimes."

Label Your Feelings (SURF)

Kept brief and in proportion, a description of your emotional reaction to the problem at hand can help elicit empathy and consideration from your loved one. Use of a feeling statement can also change the request from seeming like a demand to something more personal and important. For best results, state your feelings—or better yet, a *single* feeling—in a calm, non-accusatory manner. If your feelings are intense, it can be a good strategy to tone them down as much as possible; for example, if you're furious and terrified, you might say you feel frustrated and worried. Finally, if you can legitimately tie a positive feeling to the request, do so.

- Specific: "I'd like you to get up when your alarm goes off."
- Understanding: "I know those early mornings are tough!"
- Responsibility: "And yes, truth be told, I've made mornings more stressful by yelling at you sometimes."
- Feelings: "But if this seems doable, it'd help me feel a lot less tense at the start of the day."

Now that you've learned what SURFing involves, let's practice with these tools. After all, you can't expect perfect requests to spring from your lips automatically. And like any new skill, SURFing will probably feel awkward at first. So, use this space to plan a request you'd like to make of your loved one.

First, write out your request as you'd normally say it.

____

____

____

____

____

Now, modify your request according to **SURF**.

1. Be <u>S</u>pecific. Make a particular request of your loved one in a relatively brief sentence.

First Try	Modified
"I'm scared to death when you drink and drive. You're going to get in an accident and it's just so scary to think that could possibly happen."	"Could you find another way home other than driving if you've been drinking?"
"Can you please commit to stop smoking from now on? It's driving me crazy."	"Can we start to talk about your pot smoking and what you could do differently?"

Your specific and brief request:________________________________

____

____

2. Offer an <u>U</u>nderstanding Statement. Help your loved one feel heard and non-defensive.

First Try	Modified
"I'm not asking anything of you that I don't ask of everyone else. We all chip in."	"I know you feel rushed to get to work and don't think you have time to pick things up before you leave."
"I can't stand how much money you spend on drugs."	"I know that you feel those pills help you connect with your friends."

Your understanding statement: ________________________________

____

____

____

3. Take Partial Responsibility. You don't need to say that it's your fault (nor should you), but it's helpful to find a piece of the problem, however small, that you can share.

First Try	Modified
"It's not my job to be your maid!"	"I realize I haven't told you how much it bothers me. I can't expect you to read my mind."
"You piss me off so much when we have to talk about this again and again."	"I know I've had a short fuse when we've discussed this in the past."

Your acceptance of partial responsibility:____________________

____

____

____

4. Label Your Feelings. Identify a feeling attached to the request and describe it without being too intense or lengthy. Bonus points for also including a positive feeling.

First Try	Modified
"You push my buttons when you act so irresponsibly."	"I get concerned and upset when you have the car and I know you stopped at the bar after work."
"I'm at my wits' end."	"I get really scared when we don't have enough money for rent."

Your feeling(s) labeled:____________________________

____

____

____

Now, try putting it all together. You can play with the order and wording to make it sound as natural as possible.

____

____

____

____

____

____

____

____

Keep in mind that even the most perfectly scripted request won't guarantee the outcome you want. It will, however, increase the odds of being heard and considered. And the more you practice using tools like SURF, the easier this manner of speaking and relating to your loved one will become.

SURFing Tips

Here are a few more things to remember as you practice with this strategy:

- Start with small-ticket items or easier relationships. Practicing when the stakes are low comes in handy when they're raised.
- Again, it's helpful to write down and practice what you want to say before you say it—and to rehearse, perhaps role-playing with a friend—before you "go live." Try to anticipate your loved one's responses and fine-tune what you want to say accordingly.
- Keep in mind the timing of your conversations. Do your best to make sure your loved one is not under the influence or hungover, and that both of you are in okay moods. In other words, notice the red and green lights for both of you.

- You don't have to use every part of SURF in every interaction! However, attempting to include all of them, at least when practicing, can be helpful in getting the hang of it.

- Becoming fluent in these strategies takes practice. It's normal to feel discouraged if you make an attempt and it doesn't go well the first two or six times. Your willingness to feel discouraged and continue practicing anyway can make all the difference. We think you'll find it's worth the effort.

Putting It All Together

In this chapter, we introduced several communication tools that will make speaking to your loved one and negotiating what you want to happen easier and more productive. As we bring the chapter to an end, we want to emphasize yet again how necessary it is to practice what you're learning.

We often hear people say, "I know how to talk, and I don't want to put on some fake front!" We get that it can feel phony to try speaking a different way and that a part of you just wants to say what's really on your mind. But consider again how this has gone for you so far. In our experience, speaking one's mind often means letting a lot of pent-up emotion come blasting out, which pushes everyone further apart, toward frustration, sadness, or loneliness.

The tools and strategies in this chapter work better than the more impulsive communication that often comes naturally. Know that as you practice with them, you'll get better and sound more natural when you're using them. You'll also start to reap the benefits, as your communication has increasingly less conflict and more connection and potential for positive change.

Last but not least, know there's nothing fake about working to communicate in a more helpful way. Practicing these strategies is a loving, respectful thing for you to do. After all, the whole reason you're making this effort is because you love someone, care about them, and hope to make things better for everyone. That is an admirable pursuit.

With that, we'll move to the topic we're sure you've been waiting for: inviting your loved one to get help.

CHAPTER 8

Inviting Your Loved One to Get Help: A Special Case of Communication

Apply understanding, awareness, and communication skills to invite your loved one to get help that makes sense to them.

You've probably wanted to invite your loved one to get help for their substance use since you opened this book. Hopefully, the new understanding and tools you've gathered up to this point will help move that conversation forward. This chapter will guide you to apply understanding, awareness, and communication tools to the conversation you'd like to have with your loved one about getting help. In the next chapter, we'll provide some behavior strategies to help you support any positive steps your loved one takes, inside or outside of treatment.

A New Perspective on Getting Someone Help

Treatment can be one important part of how someone makes changes in their behavior. But we're surrounded by messages in our culture that imply treatment is the only option—messages like "Addicts have to go to rehab or they're going to die." So, it can help (and relieve pressure) to remember that there are lots of ways to get help and support and effect change that don't always include treatment.

Some people may want to get away from the consequences of consuming drugs or alcohol yet still may be hesitant, or ambivalent about getting formal treatment. Their first step might be reducing use or experimenting with abstinence on their own. Some will seek out a peer recovery support group, such as a 12-step meeting or SMART Recovery, while others will be more open to talking to a counselor. Or perhaps connecting with a certified peer mentor will feel like a good fit. Remember, one size doesn't fit all.

It's also true that professional care comes in many forms, including outpatient therapy (individual and/or group), intensive day programs (three to five days a week), sober living, inpatient residential programs and detoxes, and medications. Ideally, it also includes mental health and psychiatric care.

Ultimately, if you have a better understanding of the support options, you can make informed recommendations to your loved one and potentially lower their anxiety about what those options will look like. And as you know from the last chapter, how you share the information will affect how your loved one receives it.

To start, take a moment to think about which recommendations you might want to make to your loved one. As we've mentioned, our book *Beyond Addiction* includes a whole chapter on treatment options that may help you get the lay of the land, including these options:

- Going to a therapist
- Attending a peer support group
- Entering an outpatient or residential program
- Talking to a community elder or faith-based leader

What would you like to ask your loved one to consider doing to address their substance use?

____

____

____

How to Invite Your Loved One to Get Help

As you prepare to discuss help options with your loved one, we'll offer you some specific suggestions about how to make that go well. We'll also encourage you to use all that you've come to understand about their behavior in addition to the communication strategies you've already started to learn (LOVE, SURF). Keep the following in mind:

- Your loved one's behavior makes sense. Reflect on what they're getting from their substance use to better target the help options that may be most useful to them. If you know that they struggle with anxiety or depression, for instance, maybe they would be open to seeing a therapist to deal with those issues as a starting point. If they've stopped using substances but are feeling isolated from their friends, perhaps they'd let you take them to a self-help support group where they could meet other people.
- It's important to offer more than one option. Options increase the chances that your loved one will consider at least one of them. And don't forget, you can always ask them what they think might be helpful.
- Try to provide the information you want to share without pressure or judgment, remembering the dynamics of ambivalence. Pressuring someone to accept your

recommendations can make them defensive and more likely to argue against getting help. Pay attention to the red and green lights.

- Remember the power of positive reinforcement! Notice and compliment (for example, through affirmations) any change in efforts or openness to seeking help. (More on this in the next chapter.)

When it comes time to actually speak to your loved one about the change you'd like to help them make, try to think of reasons for seeking help—called **motivational hooks**—that are most meaningful to your loved one. Motivational hooks like these make seeking help more appealing:

- Speak directly to your loved one's interests, even if you have a specific idea about what kind of support would be best. For example, getting help for employment problems or feeling down all the time may be more important to someone than seeking treatment for alcohol use. Even though the drinking might contribute to these issues, talking about the impact of substance use on their mood, job, health, or relationships may be more acceptable to your loved one than talking about stopping use.
- Talk about what they may gain by seeking help. For example, suggesting that medication might improve their mood or energy level could be more in line with your loved one's goals than telling them medication will help them stop using.
- Think about ways to make your suggestions doable for your loved one. A small step forward can be less intimidating or threatening and result in more buy-in. So, you might propose a one-time consultation with a professional, for instance, instead of making suggestions that require more commitment, such as "starting treatment" or "getting sober." Doable could even be as simple as an offer to drive them there.

When to Invite Your Loved One to Get Help

Remember, timing matters. Pick times when the invitation is more likely to be heard or when your loved one is more likely to think about change. For instance, talking about options over coffee on a weekend morning would likely go better than after an irritating day at work.

- Look for windows of opportunity—those moments when your loved one is feeling remorse or has expressed interest in making a change. Think about when (and where) they tend to be the most approachable. Is that in the morning over coffee? After dinner? Consider what else is going on in their life so that you can pick a good time to talk.
- There are also certain times to avoid, including when they're high or hungover; are doing something that is important to them, like watching a favorite TV show or live sports; are rushing to do something else; or are irritable, tired, or not feeling well.
- Keep in mind your own emotional and physical needs and try to find a time when you're less distracted, tired, or rushed.
- Resist the urge to get an immediate answer; give your loved one some time to digest what you've suggested. They may need to mull it over before deciding what to do.
- And finally, if their response to your invitation is a "no," that's okay; it doesn't mean that all is lost. Remind yourself that this is a marathon and not a sprint. These conversations can evolve over time. The key is to stay connected and keep talking.

What Invitations to Get Help Can Look Like

Let's look at an example of an invitation to get help that uses the communication strategies we've discussed. The following script was prepared by a woman who noticed that her partner was feeling down, specifically about being unemployed. Since previous conversations about her partner's drinking had ended in yelling, she took the time to write out her invitation and practiced saying it out loud to her best friend first. Here's what she said—with the various communication strategies she used labeled, for you to see them in action.

I know losing your job was hard. You really liked the people you worked with, and it's been financially scary as well (understanding statement/validating). *I know I can be kind of sensitive* (taking partial responsibility), *but it seems like you've been drinking more on the weekends since then. It does make sense to me that you'd want to forget about work* (empathizing/recognizing behaviors make sense). *What's painful and sad for me is I feel you're forgetting about other things between us* (feeling statement). *You're usually so much fun in social situations* (affirmation) *and it upsets us both when we go out for dinner with friends and you get sleepy and don't remember the conversation later, like last night. I'd love to sit and make a list together about other things that could be helpful* (specific request). *The counselor my friend's partner sees seems like a cool guy, and he's been helping him with work stuff* (motivational hook). *Maybe we could get some other names, or you could see him once and see if he's helpful* (specific request/ providing options/suggesting one doable step). *What do you think?*

Her partner may not take her up on her suggestions. If she doesn't, there will be other chances for her to extend an invitation. Thinking of invitations to change as all-or-nothing makes the stakes higher than they need to be, and you'll be more likely to get emotional. So, practice your strategy, manage the tone of voice you use when delivering the message, be open to what you hear, and be as willing as you can to work with whatever comes. Over time, you'll have planted seeds that contribute to your loved one seeking help in some way.

Let's look at how you can structure your invitation to your loved one.

Exercise: Making the Invitation

Find motivational hooks. Try to see the problem from their point of view. Why might your loved one consider treatment or help of some sort at this time?

Examples:

- Had a car wreck
- Relationship ended
- Lost job or had to leave school

Your loved one's motivational hooks: ______________________________

____

____

What are some costs of your loved one's substance use? (Remember to focus on what's important to them.) What benefits could they experience by trying to reduce or abstain from substance use?

Examples:

Costs of using:

- Feeling down and discouraged about life
- Not being able to consistently work/have money

Benefits of seeking help/change:

- Friends are doing things they enjoy—reducing use may help them have the energy and money to participate
- Able to complete work assignments and stick to a schedule when not using

Costs of using to your loved one:

- ______________________________
- ______________________________
- ______________________________

Benefits to your loved one of seeking help/change:

- ______________________________
- ______________________________
- ______________________________

Learn from previous attempts. Think about any past attempts you've made to have these talks. What has gotten in the way of their success (e.g., timing, tone of conversation, did not provide options, was not brief)? Based on what you know now, what would you change?

Example: I got upset and told him he was in denial about how bad things were and that he had to go to meetings or rehab.

Your things to avoid: ____

____

____

Identify the red and green lights. What signals will tell you it's a good time to talk?

Signal	Timing	Situations	Moods
Red Lights			
Green Lights			

Have options available (for formal treatment and otherwise). Jot down the information here.

Treatment Option(s)	Contact Information	Wait Time

Once you've completed this exercise, you'll have laid the groundwork for the conversations you might have with your loved one about the options for help they may wish to get, considering their particular circumstances and what you and they want for their life. Now, it's time to open a notebook and start drafting your script as you'd like your part of the conversation to go. Remember to use understanding statements, affirmations, validation, and empathy, and ask for permission and accept partial responsibility where you can—communication tools proven to decrease defensiveness and increase connection and collaboration.

Then, you'll be ready for these conversations to begin.

Putting It All Together

As you plan your invitation to get help, you can see the whole ITC wheel in motion: understanding, awareness, and action. Of course, inviting your loved one to get help is just one part of your relationship as it continues to evolve. In the next chapter, we'll look at specific behavior changes you can make yourself to have a positive influence on your loved one's behavior. Know that whether you support them in getting help or encourage other kinds of positive change, your behavior shapes theirs.

CHAPTER 9

Your Behavior Shapes Theirs

Recognizing and rewarding positive change invites it to happen more, while allowing natural consequences to occur and setting respectful limits discourage negative behavior.

Ray, who takes care of his family's garden, knows that a healthy, thriving garden has many kinds of flowers and plants. He enjoys interacting with the garden and takes pride in seeing the different plants grow, from the smallest sprouts to the flowering shrubs.

But one day, Ray notices weeds beginning to grow among the flowers, including some invasive species. This concerns him. He finds himself obsessively checking the garden to see if more weeds have shown up. He starts to feel judged by neighbors and passersby. He's often distracted thinking about the weeds; sometimes he dreams about the weeds at night. Upon getting home from work, he goes straight to his backyard to pull weeds. But that doesn't work; they grow back, and so do his worries. It reaches a point when he's not really happy gardening anymore.

Finally, Ray works up the courage to ask for help. He goes to his next-door neighbor, who tells him, "Get tougher on those weeds! Cut off all the water to the garden, since putting any water on the garden at all is making the weeds grow. Once the weeds are gone, you can get back to gardening as usual."

Something about that strategy doesn't sit right. So, Ray goes to his other neighbors. "It's still important to water the flowers," they say. "How else will they survive?" Ray realizes that this was what he didn't like about the other neighbor's advice: there must be a way to support the flowers in his garden without turning his back on them. But he doesn't know about this idea either: "Shower that garden with as much water as it can take, and hopefully the flowers will grow stronger and the garden will sort itself out for the better." It seems to him the weeds will still grow—faster and out of control.

But he realizes—what if he combines approaches? "If I'm careful and water just the flowers, and I limit the growth of the weeds by withholding water and weeding those areas, perhaps I can still care for my garden, stay involved with it, and get back to enjoying it again." While this seems like hard work, he thinks it will help his garden flourish and he thinks he can be happier doing it than he has been.

Please do not take any actual gardening tips from this story. It's a metaphor. But as you try to help your loved one, you can think of yourself as a gardener whose goal is to help them develop a varied, healthy behavioral garden in which they can thrive and find their way. In this chapter, you'll learn to use tools to cultivate the behaviors you want to see more of (the flowers) while implementing behavior-reducing strategies so that destructive behaviors (the weeds) are weakened, reduced, or eliminated over time.

Cultivating a behavioral garden takes effort—Ray was right about that. You'll use many of the ideas and strategies you've learned thus far. Throughout this chapter, we spotlight helpful ways to combine understanding, awareness, and action. Ultimately, it's the combination of everything in the Invitation to Change—the whole wheel—that will help you nurture a beautiful, diverse behavioral garden for you and your loved one to enjoy together.

Behavior Strategy #1: Use Positive Reinforcement to Encourage Change

It's natural to focus on destructive and scary behaviors like substance use, intoxication, fighting, poor school performance, not having a job, being argumentative, and risky behavior, to name just a few. And it's likely that your loved one's unhealthy behavior gets most if not all your attention—even when they aren't using substances—because you're (understandably) still fuming about the last time they lost control, or you're worried about the next. You may find yourself in a cycle of lecturing, threatening, or punishing your loved one as you try to get them to stop behaving in this way.

Unfortunately, when your loved one mostly receives negative attention, it means that the behaviors you'd like to see are getting ignored, and opportunities for change are lost. This is akin to Ray's not watering anything in the garden, including the flowers. Your loved one may think, since they "can't do anything right" and everyone is obviously upset all the time, why bother changing?

The reality is that flowers need water and behaviors need **positive reinforcement** to keep growing. Science has shown that if we notice someone's positive behaviors when they happen, and let them know we see them, we can support, strengthen, and increase those behaviors, which helps them along the path to change (Iguchi et al. 1997; Petry 2012).

Remember that your loved one's behavior makes sense to them. In other words, something about it is reinforcing, which makes them want to continue it. Thankfully, you can use reinforcement to help other behaviors make sense to them, too.

Research has proven time and again that positive reinforcement works to help people change their relationship to substances (Ginley et al. 2021; Higgins et al. 2004; Azrin 1976). Substance use (and other compulsive behaviors) affects the brain and body and feels good in the short term. Substances also work quickly and are therefore powerful reinforcers. When we want to help someone decrease or stop such behaviors, we must find ways to compete with their reinforcing effects. That is, we must find other reinforcers—other behaviors that have positive effects.

This is where you come in. You can help your loved one find alternative rewarding things to do and, critically, your own behavior can be one of the positive effects of doing those things instead of using substances. When you reinforce your loved one's constructive behaviors, like coming home sober, it makes it more likely the behavior will happen again. And whether the reinforcement is internal (they feel satisfied with themselves) or external—either from you (you smile and thank them) or someone/something else (they get a paycheck)—the behavior that gets a positive response is more likely to be repeated. Positive reinforcement helps them learn to feel good in ways unrelated to using drugs or alcohol. Noticing and rewarding your loved one's healthy behavioral choices has a number of benefits: they can feel proud of themselves, acknowledged, and recognized for their efforts; they don't suffer the punishing effects of that substance; and they reap the rewards of the new healthy behavior, such as feeling healthier! They can start to compare and contrast what using looks and feels like to all the benefits of sobriety (or reduced use). All of this can contribute to an increased sense of self-worth and improved ability to cope with life.

What Positive Reinforcement Looks Like

You can think of reinforcing behavior in an intentional way—watering the parts of the garden you want to see grow—in three steps: noticing, acknowledging, and responding.

1. To reinforce a behavior, first we have to notice it. Noticing, or actively looking for the behaviors you want to support, can be a challenge, especially when they occur in the midst of negative behaviors or while other things are competing for your attention. It may be hard to see the flowers for the weeds, particularly if the flowers are small. The important thing is that you're helping to create an environment where your loved one begins to feel more open, more accepted, less hostile, and more connected. Changes in substance use can take time to follow once this shift starts to occur, but you can still appreciate the positive shift.

2. Then, we can acknowledge the behavior. Acknowledging means noting to yourself and the other person that you saw them doing good. Positive moments can be

fleeting, and your attention can get quickly pulled away. However, saying to yourself that your loved one was home on time or spoke nicely to you helps put a verbal stamp on it. This can build momentum in noticing the positives.

3. Finally, we choose how to respond to the behavior. Responding is an intentional, reinforcing reaction to someone's behavior. This could be with a verbal acknowledgment (attention and affirmations are reinforcers too!) or by providing a reward. Responding in this way not only increases the likelihood that your loved one will repeat the behavior, but it also contributes to a sense that their world can be rewarding when sober.

Note: It is not reinforcing if you reward before the behavior happens. Resist the temptation to give something now in the hopes that their behavior will change later. That turns what should be a reinforcing reward into a bribe.

Isn't This Enabling?

You've probably heard that if you do anything to directly support someone while they're using, you're enabling them. In addition to some of these ideas not actually being so helpful, they probably make you feel pretty bad about your loved one and yourself!

Positive reinforcement is something different. Unlike enabling, positive reinforcement is not about pretending that everything is okay. Think of positive reinforcement as watering the flowers in your garden but not the weeds, whereas enabling is watering everything indiscriminately, reinforcing the behavior you don't want along with the behavior you do want. With positive reinforcement, the idea is to catch your loved one doing good, as rare as that may seem at times.

Try to step back and look at the larger picture to find any positive behaviors you can reinforce. For example, if you notice a rare day that your loved one is sober, or that they got up in the morning and went to work without your prodding, tell them that you appreciate it. Let's take a moment to consider specific behaviors your loved one does that you might like to see change, alternatives you could reinforce, and ways you could make the request to them, using the SURF strategy you learned in chapter 8.

Exercise: Getting Started with Reinforcement

Identify behaviors. List the behaviors your loved one engages in that you'd like to see change, then identify a specific, alternative healthy behavior you'd like to support in its place. Which flowers do you want to water?

Behavior to Change (want to decrease)	Alternative Behavior to Reinforce (want to increase)
Falling asleep in front of the TV every night drinking	Watching a show together, without drinking Helping the kids with their homework
Continuing to use opiates despite ODing	Agreeing to a medication consultation Training girlfriend and parent in overdose reversal procedures
Coming home from school late and stoned	Coming home on time Coming home sober
Getting up late and making the morning stressful for everyone	Getting up on time Acting in a more cooperative manner

Identify rewards. Brainstorm rewards to reinforce the healthy behaviors above. Here are some points to keep in mind as you brainstorm:

- Rewards are in the eye of the beholder. A dinner at your favorite restaurant might feel special to you, but for them, a gift card from a store they like might hit closer to the mark. Spend some time thinking and even talking to them about what they find rewarding. You can also look around for what rewards they're already getting that you might want to tie to their positive behavior.
- Rewards fit your loved one's needs in their current life stage; these may change as they develop. For example, most ten-year-olds prize quality time with a parent, but at seventeen, not so much. Similarly, a night out with friends "like old times" seems like a fun way to connect with your partner, but may be the exact opposite of what they want after a week of work and taking care of the kids.
- Rewards should be consistent and closely follow the behavior they're meant to strengthen. Timing helps link the reward to the behavior, so plan rewards that you can deliver immediately or shortly after the behavior takes place. Remember not to reward ahead of time in the hopes that the behavior will change later—bribery is less effective. Positive behavior is also more powerfully reinforced if rewards are reliable instead of random. If you greet your partner warmly when they come home sober only to be surly the next time because you're upset about something else, the reinforcement of coming home sober will be slower to develop.
- Rewards are things you're willing and able to give. Choose rewards within your budget that expose your loved one to healthy activities and communities. The rewards you choose should also feel comfortable and consistent with your values. If a gift feels like too much, or a gesture doesn't feel genuine, or words don't feel honest, keep brainstorming until you identify a reward that is both reinforcing to your loved one and natural for you. Some of the most effective rewards, like your attention, compliments, and affection, are free.

Here are some examples of rewards—both free rewards and those that cost something:

Free Rewards	Rewards That Cost Something
If he helps with the kids' homework, I'll let him know what a loving dad I think he is.	If he watches TV with me sober this week, I'll treat him to the movie he's wanted us to go see.
If she agrees to talk to a doctor about medication options, I'll cook her favorite dinner that night.	If she gets an overdose reversal kit for the house, I'll get her a new phone.
If they come home on time, I'll offer to walk the dog while they relax.	If they come home on time, I'll order their favorite takeout.

From there, develop a reinforcer menu. Take a moment to list rewards that you can provide after the positive behavior you want to support occurs:

- Reinforcers that cost something: ______________________________

  ____

- Reinforcers that are an activity: ______________________________

  ____

- Reinforcers that are free: ______________________________

  ____

- Reinforcers using words: ______________________________

  ____

SURF your request. Use the information you gathered in the previous steps to draft a specific request you'd like to make of your loved one—and a specific behavior you want to reinforce—using the SURF communication strategy. Name behaviors you'd like to see more of and the reinforcement that will occur if they honor the request. We start with an example of a request without SURF, and then modify the request using SURF. Then, it's your turn to form a SURF request.

As a reminder, SURF involves:

- Being <u>S</u>pecific
- Offering an <u>U</u>nderstanding Statement
- Taking Partial <u>R</u>esponsibility
- Labeling Your <u>F</u>eelings

Be <u>S</u>pecific. Identify the precise behavior you want to see increase or decrease in as few words as possible.

First Try	Modified
"Don't talk to me that way."	"I'd appreciate it if you'd lower your voice and use nicer words in our conversation."
"We don't want you sitting around the house all day. You should be doing something more useful."	"We'd like you to spend time looking for a job."

Your specific request: ____

____

____

Next, also be specific in describing the reinforcement/reward that will follow the behavior. In as few words as possible, tell your loved one how you will respond to the behavior if it occurs.

First Try	Modified
"Help us out by bringing out the garbage tonight."	"I'd appreciate it if you'd take out the garbage tonight; to show my appreciation, I'll give you more time tomorrow to play video games."
"Why don't you help me with the dishes?"	"If you help me with the dishes, I'll give you a break from the kids."

Your statement outlining the specific reinforcement: ______________________________

____

____

Offer an Understanding Statement. Help your loved one feel heard and non-defensive.

First Try	Modified
"Why are you always complaining? You should be grateful for ____________."	"I know making changes can be hard, and sometimes it seems easier to give up."
"You have to be more responsible. You shouldn't be going out with your friends at the bar."	"I know you like going out with your friends on the weekend, and it's important to have a social life."

Your understanding statement: ______________________________

____

____

Take Partial Responsibility. Remember, this is not admitting fault, but it's helpful to find a piece of the problem, however small, that you can share.

First Try	Modified
"You need to be more respectful when you talk to me."	"I realize I can get pretty heated in our conversations about this. I will practice listening more than shouting."
"You should have told me about this earlier."	"I know I've been really busy lately and less available to talk."

Your acceptance of partial responsibility: ______________________________

____

____

Label Your Feelings. Identify a feeling attached to the request and describe it without being too intense or lengthy. Bonus points for also including a positive feeling.

First Try	Modified
"I've been up all night worried sick since I couldn't get ahold of you!"	"I love you and get concerned when you don't answer your phone or respond to my texts."
"You just talk over me, you never listen!"	"I get frustrated when I'm not given the opportunity to voice my opinion."

Your feeling(s) labeled: ____

____

____

Putting it all together. You can play with the order and wording to make it sound as natural as possible. Keep in mind that even the most perfectly scripted request won't guarantee the outcome you want. It will, however, increase the odds of being heard—and of the new behavior occurring.

Your whole SURF request:

____

____

____

____

____

____

Strategically reinforcing constructive behaviors in this way will help sustain your loved one's motivation over the long haul. Reinforcement, done well and consistently, impacts their internal motivation because, as they experience the benefits of the new behavior, it becomes rewarding in and of itself.

Reinforcement also gives you permission to stay connected and deliver positive messages instead of always being the negative person in your loved one's life, a person they want to avoid. This can help both of you feel better; it could change the whole tone of your relationship.

Finally, understanding the value of positive reinforcement will help you counter the common cultural message that the only way to help is to detach and punish—metaphorically, to cut off all the water. Watering the flowers that you want to support is not enabling or being codependent, unless "enabling" means enabling the behaviors you want! The key is to be thoughtful about what you water, and how.

Troubleshooting Reinforcement

Positive reinforcement strategies aim to increase positive behavior—and this can take time, since you and your loved one have a history around these issues. Gardens take time. Weeds keep cropping up while the flowers, shrubs, and trees you want take time to sprout, take root, and grow. So, let's work through some of the issues that might arise as you begin working to reinforce new adaptive behaviors.

The reinforcement I try doesn't seem to work. If you try reinforcing positive behaviors and you *don't* see an increase in a behavior or positive change over time, consider these questions:

- How long after the behavior did my reinforcement occur? Or was it not provided at all?
- How did I deliver the reinforcer, if I gave one? Did the tone of my voice and the words that I used communicate that I appreciated the behavior? What could I change about the delivery?
- Have I missed the occurrence of the behavior(s)? Am I clear about what I'm looking for? How would I recognize it?
- Was the reward not desired by my loved one (and thus not really a reinforcer for them)? What reward would be more desirable?

- If I requested the behavior change, did I use SURF tools to make the request? Was it clear, or did my loved one think the reward was tied to a different behavior?

Ultimately, success with positive reinforcement requires good communication. How reinforcement is delivered is just as important as what is being delivered. How would you react if a pizza deliverer threw the pizza at your door instead of handing it to you? Would that be appetizing? Communication is a critical part of reinforcing behavior.

Also remember that change is about adding new behaviors, not subtracting or erasing old behaviors. As we discussed in the chapter on ambivalence, people cannot magically forget what they've already learned. When someone engages in behaviors that you'd like to see decrease or stop, think instead about the behaviors you'd like to see introduced or increased. For example, if your loved one avoids talking to you because every conversation ends in an argument, try having a conversation about a neutral topic they raised. Talking to you is, in that moment, the opposite of sitting in their room alone or doing something negative, such as using drugs or alcohol; it's a competing and positive behavior. Plus, a positive interaction with you can open a new pathway for more conversations in the future. Providing reinforcement encourages and strengthens those positive behaviors.

This is too hard. Using reinforcement strategies to support your loved one's new behaviors can feel like a lot of work, especially when change is slow to take hold. It's crucial to bring in other elements of ITC—namely self-awareness, willingness, and self-compassion. There can be moments when it's really hard. Does any of the following feel familiar?

I'm so pissed about what has happened over the past week!

I'm so tired today!

I'm scared!

You expect me to reinforce "good" behaviors when he's still using?!

At times, positive reinforcement can feel emotionally unfulfilling, as in:

Why should I provide rewards for things she should be doing anyway?

I've had a lousy day and don't feel like being nice.

I've tried this before and I'm just not good at it.

She's the one with the problem and I'm the one doing all the work. When is she *going to reinforce* me?

As the person providing the reinforcement, you matter too. Using self-awareness to recognize thoughts and feelings are present and taking them as signals to guide your response can be helpful. Pressing pause allows you to check in with yourself and your willingness in the moment, to ask yourself these questions:

- *Why is it important to me to provide reinforcement?*
- *How is this in service of supporting my loved one?*
- *How do I want to be in this relationship?*
- *What values do I want to put into action in this situation?*
- *Is there something I could also be doing to help me?*

And don't forget to practice a little self-compassion. Notice how you talk to yourself and allow some room to be human in the moment. Checking in with yourself can help reinforce your efforts by reminding you how meaningful they are!

What if my loved one is a teen? If your loved one is a teen or young adult, change can be even bumpier, as they're in constant flux developmentally. In fact, brain development continues up to our mid-twenties, especially in those areas that we associate with self-control and decision-making. Try to tolerate the process, know that reinforcement is a powerful change agent even at this age, and remember that changing behavior patterns takes a willingness to resist engaging in old habits long enough to learn new ones. It's a lot of work!

What if my loved one isn't living at home? It's true that reinforcement is most effective when you're around to see the behavior you want to encourage. When you have significantly less contact with your loved one—for instance, when they don't live with you—circumstances change a bit. You don't have as much access to them and their behaviors, so you won't be available to reinforce positive behavior as immediately or as often or consistently. But even here, there are options for reinforcement—reaching out to them, rewarding them with recognition and praise for behavior changes they make, showing you care and recognize the progress they're making—and reinforcement will still be a way to strengthen new behaviors. Try to be creative about the ways you keep the connection open, the conversation going, and the information flowing. An affirmation can be just as, if not more, powerful by text, since they'll have it in writing to reread whenever they could use encouragement.

Of course, catching your loved one doing good, watering the parts of their behavioral garden that you want to grow, is made all the more effective by how you respond to their negative behaviors as well. This brings us to the second behavior strategy: allowing natural consequences—the world, essentially—to be your loved one's teacher.

Behavior Strategy #2: Allow Natural Consequences to Take Their Course

You've likely felt the impulse to help your loved one keep up with their responsibilities or take better care of themselves, like calling work to cover for your partner when they're too hungover to go, or giving your child money to get by after they've spent their savings on drugs or alcohol. Unfortunately, in trying to help this way, you often (unintentionally) reinforce or support substance use or negative behaviors. This is like watering the weeds. Naturally, you want to smooth the rough edges, but this prevents your loved one from learning from the outcomes of their own choices. When you shield someone from the uncomfortable results of their actions, you remove the downside to their behaviors. And this becomes yet another way in which their behaviors make sense to them. If they're getting something they like from doing what they're doing (reduced pain or increased pleasure or both) and they aren't experiencing much downside, why wouldn't they continue those behaviors?

Allowing **natural consequences** (failed grades, missed social events, a cold supper) and the next strategy, setting limits, will help you reduce negative behaviors, just as positive reinforcement will increase positive ones.

What Are Natural Consequences?

Natural consequences are the unwanted costs that organically happen as a result of substance use. These are outcomes that your loved one would experience if no one interfered. They are the opposite of positive reinforcement because they discourage the behavior that led to them. Remember that behaviors make sense: when we put our hand on a hot stove, the consequence is burned skin and pain, and this deters us from putting our hand on a hot stove in the future.

Behaviors that aren't rewarding or that have significant undesirable natural consequences tend to decrease or stop. Allowing natural consequences, then, is the practice of not interfering when your loved one experiences them. Here are some examples of natural consequences:

- Negative physical outcomes, such as hangovers, headaches, digestive problems, skin problems, dental problems, withdrawal, increased tolerance
- Psychological-emotional costs, such as depression, shame, feeling out of control, not feeling satisfied with how life is going
- Behavioral costs, such as sleep disruption, poor nutrition, injuries
- Life costs, such as disruption or loss of relationships, financial problems, legal problems

Natural consequences are distinct from imposed consequences, or punishment. You've probably heard about or tried many ways to punish or "get rid of" substance use, depending on the age of your loved one. If you're a parent or caregiver, you may have tried grounding, time-outs, withdrawing financial support, lecturing, or yelling. If you're a partner or spouse, you may have tried limiting the time you spend together, taking control of the finances, yelling, lecturing, or withholding affection. Some of these are in the category of punishment, and all of them are delivered by you.

In contrast, natural consequences let the world teach the lesson. The world can be a powerful teacher if you let it! The trick is to allow natural consequences to speak for themselves. For instance, the teen who stays out too late, misses an important test, and maybe fails a class has experienced a natural consequence for her actions. By allowing such consequences to occur, you will help your loved one understand that their behavior is a choice that has outcomes they may not like—and that those outcomes are not determined by you; they're the products of your loved one's own behavior. If instead, you attempt to deliver these lessons through your own actions or reactions, you shift the negative focus to you.

With this behavioral strategy, there are some important distinctions to make. Natural consequences are *not* "tough love." They are not intended to shame or hurt someone.

Instead, you're letting your loved one experience the direct connection between their actions and those costs—which makes them more likely to reduce or stop those actions.

When you positively reinforce healthy behaviors and allow natural consequences to play out, you end up with a potent mixture. Your loved one will experience the connection between positive behavior and outcomes while feeling the impact of natural consequences of their negative behaviors. They can then decide which they want more of, costs or rewards.

And, if you're going to say it, do make sure that you're okay to follow through with it. If the behavior (say, oversleeping) happens, the natural consequence (for example, missing work) must be allowed to happen for the teaching moment to occur. If you doubt you can follow through, that's okay! It simply means that this isn't a workable natural consequence to choose at this time, in which case it's better for you to not say anything at all.

Exercise: Practicing Allowing Natural Consequences

It's not easy to stand by and allow natural consequences to occur. We're geared to protect the people we love from pain, even in times when they're the source of that pain. The goal of this exercise is to help prepare you for this difficult task.

1. Think about some specific natural consequences that your loved one may experience because of their substance use. Focus on "safe-to-allow" consequences. (If you're wondering how to distinguish which consequences are safe to allow and which aren't, know that we'll discuss that in more detail later in the chapter.)
2. Examine whether there's anything you're tempted to do to buffer or soften the downsides/natural consequences of their behavior.
3. List the consequences you could safely let happen. Also, consider who else in your family would need to be on board to allow these same consequences—otherwise, there's a hole in the teaching bucket!

1. Potential/Actual Natural Consequences of Loved One's Use (Focus on "safe-to-allow" consequences.)	2. Actions That Buffer/ Soften the Consequences	3. Actions That Would Allow Natural Consequences
Staying out late and doing cocaine, missing work after sleeping in, feeling ill	Going to his room several times to make sure he gets up on time, offering to drive him to work, making things easier because he's not feeling well (being extra quiet, bringing food, or aspirin)	Letting him oversleep and have to talk to his boss about why he didn't show up on time
Getting drunk at dinner with friends, saying embarrassing things that he doesn't remember later, friends expressing concern	Staying through dinner despite getting increasingly upset, acting as go-between by telling him how friends feel	Leaving dinner early if uncomfortable with how he's behaving, encouraging friends to tell him directly what they observed and how they feel
Spending money on weekend partying, not having money to pay a bill	Lending money so she won't have to deal with a late payment fee or loss of service	Not lending money to pay the bill, or lending money or paying the bill only to reward positive behavior

Who in your family would need to be on board to allow these consequences to happen? What might need to happen to get them on board?

____

____

____

____

____

Exercise: Collaboratively Communicating Natural Consequences

Communicating your intentions ahead of time can help your loved one's learning process as they experience natural consequences—and SURF is a great communication strategy for this type of discussion.

In the example below, you'll see how the speaker communicates the specific behavior they want to encourage and the natural consequence that will result if it doesn't happen, as well as statements that provide understanding, take partial responsibility, and identify feelings.

I understand hanging out with friends is important to you (understanding statement) *and that you may meet up with them at the bar tonight. You have work tomorrow. In the past, I've been frustrated* (feeling statement) *when you oversleep, and I've tried to get you up or I wind up calling your work to let them know you won't be there. I know it's been my choice to do this* (partial responsibility). *I wanted to let you know that I won't be doing that anymore. I'll leave it to you to get up and get to work on time* (specific desired behavior). *I will not wake you up if you oversleep* (natural consequences).

Remember, it's important to state your position plainly and to be consistent.

Choose one of the situations that you wrote about in the previous worksheet. Using SURF, craft a paragraph informing your loved one of the change in how you will respond.

____

____

____

____

Safety and Impact on Others

Of course, some consequences are too harmful for you and/or your loved one to allow. As you consider how to let natural consequences play a role, think through the painful realities (both internal/emotional and external/concrete) that may result, and decide whether there are lines you just don't want to cross.

Some consequences will be out of your control, regardless of whether you'd choose to allow them. Others you may get to determine. For example, allowing your loved one to sleep late and risk losing their job may mean losing an important source of revenue for your family—but you may decide that you are willing to take that risk and you'll be able to navigate whatever might happen as a result. On the other hand, if your loved one chooses to drive home intoxicated, they could hurt or even kill someone—and such natural consequences may be ones you just cannot allow. That's okay. Make each decision in the context of your family, your values, the knowledge you have of your loved one, and the imperative to keep them and others safe. On occasions when you need to block a certain consequence for reasons of safety, you can turn to other strategies to express your concerns, like reinforcing healthy behaviors or using communication strategies. You can also use the next strategy, setting limits, to help you sort out what you can and cannot tolerate.

Behavior Strategy #3: Setting Limits and Planning Consequences

Natural consequences won't always be sufficiently motivating in and of themselves. Even though someone may not like some of the natural consequences associated with their substance use, they'll likely still be ambivalent about change, because some part of their old behaviors still makes sense to them. They may decide to continue using despite the negative impacts on their physical and emotional well-being, financial security, and relationships.

If your loved one is or has ever been in this position, you may understandably feel that nothing matters to them. Thankfully, even when it feels this way, it's not true. Motivation and change remain possible—particularly when you make clear to your loved one the limits to what you'll tolerate.

The goal of setting limits is not to punish them, but to reduce a certain behavior and protect yourself emotionally from it if it does occur. Establishing a limit is not the same as giving an ultimatum, nor is it a threat. Instead, clarifying your limit for yourself and the other person lets them know the outcome of their choices in advance: "If you choose to do A, then I will do B; if you choose X instead, then I will do Y." By matter-of-factly explaining the outcome of their choices ahead of time, you set the stage for your loved one to take account of their own decisions.

Setting Limits/Planning Consequences Creates Conditions for Change

While neither of the two "behavior-reducing" strategies—allowing natural consequences and setting limits—is a silver bullet, they're part of creating conditions for change.

Limit-setting is a direct act of compassion toward yourself! Taking the time to check in with yourself, to notice what is tolerable and self-respecting and what is not, is an important part of navigating and sustaining change. Setting limits is about realizing that you can say "no more" to certain things, and that your goal is, again, not just to reduce certain behaviors your loved one engages in, but also to protect yourself if they do occur.

Defining a limit is tapping into your self-compassion and concluding, "Yes, going forward, I will step away from this type of interaction or behavior, and I will be clear ahead of time to the other person that this will be the consequence." This is the equivalent of redirecting the hose and not watering the weeds.

As a consequence, it also removes a reinforcer—your compassionate, loving presence in your loved one's life. And this allows you to bring that reinforcer back when the desired behavior shows up again. By communicating your limits in advance and delivering positive reinforcement for healthy behaviors, you'll be better able to maintain a balanced, rewarding relationship with your loved one in the long run.

Aversive Strategies Don't Work (In the Long Run)

When it comes to setting limits and responding to behaviors that you don't want to encourage, keep in mind that control strategies such as shouting, screaming, lecturing, or inflicting emotional or physical pain do not reduce or stop negative behaviors. Ineffective responses also include shaming ("You disgust me"), criticizing ("You never get it right!"), and labeling ("You're such an addict"). These responses are usually driven by emotions such as fear, anger, and frustration. In the moment, **aversive strategies** like these may feel reasonable or relieving. But they come with several important downsides worth keeping in mind:

- They often wound the other person emotionally, fracture communication, and damage your connection. They're likely to reduce your loved one's willingness to learn new things or be influenced by you, providing you with less opportunity to reinforce and support positive behaviors.
- You may hope that these strategies will make your loved one want to avoid the behavior you're reacting to, but they'll be more inclined to avoid you instead.
- People build a tolerance to these types of negative consequences, especially if they're also getting something positive from the behavior. When the unwanted behavior starts up again, you'll be backed into a corner, as you feel pressure to up the ante and increase the pain. This becomes a vicious and unhelpful cycle for everyone.
- At best, these strategies work only in the short run and do not promote long-term change.

Remember, we can't erase old behaviors; they always have the potential to come back. The key is to help your loved one build a repertoire of new behaviors that make it less likely they'll default to the old ones.

That said, there will likely be times when things get out of hand or explosive, either in your loved one's behavior or in your state of mind. In such moments, giving yourself permission to simply step away can be a powerful strategy—and it may be the best thing for your own health and safety.

PAUSE BUTTON: STEPPING AWAY

Stepping away, sometimes literally as in "walk away," reduces the amount of reinforcement to zero and lets the other person know that you're not interested in engaging with them when they act a certain way. For example, you can decide not to have a conversation with them when they're being rude or verbally aggressive. You can decide not to spend any time with them when they're altered by substances. When you step away, you remove social reinforcement—you—while giving yourself space to think about how you want to respond to the behavior instead of reacting in the moment. Pressing the pause button like this can cool things down for both of you, preventing the situation from derailing further. Most importantly, permission to step away is permission you can give yourself in the moment. It's helpful to communicate limits ahead of time when you can, but stepping away if you feel the need is something you can just do for yourself, planned or not.

How to Set Limits

Let's explore the steps for setting limits now.

Identify your boundaries and the behavior that crosses them. Take some time to think about specific behaviors and interactions with your loved one that are not acceptable to you. When a boundary gets crossed, it's easy to become provoked and to label the whole person as irresponsible, entitled, spoiled, etcetera, rather than concentrating on the specific behavior that is unacceptable. Clearly define the behavior(s) that crosses your boundaries. This step builds on the awareness tools you gathered in part 2, in that it requires you to slow down and pay attention to your thoughts, feelings, and values.

As you clarify your boundaries, keep in mind that your loved one probably does many things that, while painful, are different from behaviors you absolutely cannot accept. There will be times when being uncomfortable or upset is part of staying connected to the things you value and times when it calls for a limit to be set. Compare the following two scenarios:

My partner is mad about his relapse. He's cursing and stomping around, feeling upset with himself, and just needs to vent. Part of me is frightened by his behavior—but he's not threatening me in any way; he's expressing his frustration with himself. I want to stick to my values of being present and connected and not remove myself from the situation, because it helps him feel not so alone in his struggle.

versus

My partner is mad about his relapse. He's cursing and stomping around, feeling upset with himself. His venting has turned into cursing at me and blaming me for the relapse! I want to stick to my values of being present and connected and not remove myself from the situation, because it helps him feel not so alone in his struggle; however, I find it unacceptable to be cursed at and treated disrespectfully. I let him know that I am going for a drive to my sister's, which is what I had told him I'd do if he started to act this way.

In the first example, the speaker's boundaries have not been crossed: the partner's behavior is not in violation of the speaker's personal values of safety or self-respect. The second example, however, shows a reason to set a limit. You can see how limit-setting helps discourage negative behaviors and allows you to treat yourself with compassion and respect. Calmly following through on the agreed-upon consequences lets you stay true to your values while inserting intention and consistency into an otherwise chaotic situation.

Plan your response. Think about how you want to respond to the behavior that crosses your boundary and identify the reinforcer you will remove in response to that behavior. Here are some tips on planning your response:

- Identify an alternative behavior. Specify the behavior you want to see in place of the one that crosses your boundary. Remember, change happens through addition. What flowers would you like to help grow?

- Remove meaningful reinforcers. Make sure, too, that the removal matches the severity of the behavior. In other words, don't go straight for the biggest hammer (for example, "You're grounded for life" or "I'm leaving you"). And remember, what is meaningful to your loved one may change over time.
- Remove a reward as close to the unwanted behavior as possible. The more immediate the consequence, the stronger the teaching moment.
- Identify rewards that you're willing and able to remove. Threatening to kick your loved one out of the house without being prepared to change the locks will only reduce your credibility, which is something you want to keep intact.
- Plan when you'll add reinforcement back in. Identify the specific behavior you'd want to see for you to add the positive reinforcer back in. Remember, it's most effective to combine behavior-reducing strategies with behavior-growing strategies.

Communicate clearly. When possible, let the other person know your limit ahead of time. This allows limit-setting to be less emotional and more of a learning experience in the long run. Using LOVE and SURF tools will help you explain your limits in a way that your loved one can hear.

Follow your plan. One of the least helpful things you can do is to set a limit around negative behaviors and then backtrack. Be sure to set only limits you're actually willing to enforce. Following through is crucial for limit-setting to work as a strategy.

Be consistent. Consistency in action means the removal of reinforcement is upheld by everyone (e.g., mom *and* dad) and continues over time, not only on certain days or when you remember. Fatigue, the need to tend to other responsibilities and relationships, and your emotions in the moment can all make maintaining consistency difficult. Reminding yourself why you're setting limits and practicing positive communication will help you stay the course.

Exercise: Practicing Setting Limits and Planning Consequences

In this exercise, you'll practice identifying boundaries, setting limits, or planning consequences for when those boundaries are crossed, and communicating all of this to your loved one using the SURF strategy.

1. Identify your boundaries and a behavior that may cross it. The behavior should be one that you'd like to see decreased.
2. Identify a healthy alternative you'd like to see in its place. What reinforcer(s) could you remove in response to the unwanted behavior and give back when the healthy alternative occurs?
3. How would you communicate this to your loved one? Remember to SURF: be Specific, offer Understanding, take partial Responsibility, and label your Feeling(s).

See the following table for some examples of this process in action.

Behavior(s) You Would Like to See Reduced + Healthy Alternative	Reinforcer to Withdraw/ Reinstate	How to Communicate the Consequence (SURF)
Behavior: Staying out late, past 2 a.m., with the car (he's supposed to be back by 2 a.m.) **Healthy Alternative:** Being in the house by 2 a.m. when he borrows the car	**Removal:** Access to the car can be withdrawn for a period of time. **Reinstate:** Access to the car can be offered when the wanted behaviors occur (such as being home on time).	"I know it's hard to leave when your friends are hanging out, but we discussed that when you have the car, you're to be home by 2. If you're more than fifteen minutes late, you won't be able to use the car next weekend. I'm happy to send a reminder text if that would be helpful."
Behavior: Speaking loudly and in a harsh tone when he needs money to cover his bills **Healthy Alternative:** Speaking at a lower volume and with a nicer tone	**Removal:** I can tell him how I prefer to be spoken to and remove myself from the conversation. **Reinstate:** I can provide my attention and listen if spoken to in a more polite manner.	"I know you're stressed, and I'd like to be supportive. I'm not okay, however, with being spoken to in a rude way. If you can't speak to me in a softer tone and less demanding way, I will be stepping away from the conversation."

Your Turn

Behavior(s) You Would Like to See Reduced + Healthy Alternative	Reinforcer to Withdraw/ Reinstate	How to Communicate the Consequence (SURF)
Behavior: Healthy Alternative:	Removal: Reinstate:	
Behavior: Healthy Alternative:	Removal: Reinstate:	
Behavior: Healthy Alternative:	Removal: Reinstate:	

SURFing to Set Limits: Ibram and Keisha

To help you see the process of setting limits in action, we'll consider the case of Ibram. Ibram is the father of Keisha, a twenty-two-year-old who recently moved back home after graduating from college. He worries about Keisha; he sees that she hasn't been acting like herself, staying out very late drinking with friends several times per week, sleeping into the afternoons, being irritable and lethargic, and showing no interest in finding a job. Meanwhile, Ibram has been putting in a lot of overtime at work and has not been home as much as he'd like.

Recently, Ibram had reason to believe that Keisha drove home while intoxicated. He notices that he's angry, scared, and worried about her safety, health, and future. He also feels bad after they argue, knowing that he hasn't been present and worrying he's dropping the ball as a father. He wants to talk to her about drinking and driving, but every time he tries, the conversation ends in yelling.

Ultimately, Ibram decides that he needs to set limits. If Keisha's been drinking and needs a ride home, he'll be willing to drive her or figure out some other way to get her home, even if she went out using the family car. But if she's been drinking and she decides to drive herself, she'll lose the privilege of using the car for the week. Ibram uses SURF to script a conversation with Keisha:

> *Keisha, the other night when it seemed like you drove home intoxicated, I felt really scared* (labeling feelings). *I know that it hasn't been easy for you since you came back from school* (understanding statement). *I also know that I've been working a lot, so it may not seem like I'm available to help* (partial responsibility). *But the next time you've been drinking and you need to come home, please call me first* (specific request). *I can help you figure out a safe way to get home. If you do drive home intoxicated, you'll lose the privilege of using the car for the week* (setting limit).

He also thinks about how he'll respond to different outcomes, role-playing various situations with his wife. Notice how he incorporates other elements of ITC (like awareness, self-compassion, and reinforcement) in this plan:

If Keisha gets defensive, I'll hit the pause button and remind myself that I need to be supportive and patient, because that's important to me. I'll try to keep calm, and if she tells me to leave, I will step away after letting her know it's important to speak about this and asking when today would be a better time. If she listens and continues the conversation, I'll reinforce the listening by stating my appreciation for her talking about this with me.

Ibram also takes the additional step of considering the best time to have this conversation, ruling out mornings (when he's rushing out the door) and Wednesdays (when he faces several meetings with his boss and is already on edge). He seeks support from his wife as he practices.

Putting It All Together

Keep in mind Ray and his garden as you go about tending to yours and helping your loved one with theirs. With positive reinforcement, you can cultivate the flowers you want to see in your and your loved one's life. By allowing natural consequences and setting limits, you can protect the flowers and avoid feeding the weeds. The botanical principles of the metaphor may be questionable, but we assure you the behavioral principles of these strategies are sound.

As you no doubt noticed as you began to practice, in real life these strategies use the whole ITC wheel. You'll need to understand your loved one's behavior and what does or doesn't work for your loved one in a given situation, at a given point in their change process, to decide which consequences to set or allow. You'll need to use communication strategies like SURF and LOVE to implement behavior strategies like positive reinforcement and limit-setting, to invite your loved one to get help, and to share your new understanding. And you'll need awareness, willingness, and self-compassion as your guiding lights through it all. But if you can do this with patience and persistence, you will see results. You can always reread sections of this guide or revisit exercises when you need a refresher.

This brings us to the subject of the final chapter of this book: practice.

CONCLUSION

Practice, Practice, Practice

Perhaps you've seen your loved one take steps forward and then return to old behaviors again. Remember, what you're dealing with is hard; it's also the product of, potentially, years of old experience and learning. Change won't happen overnight or in ways you can predict. Practice and persistence are key. There's no such thing as too much practice when you're learning and growing, as we hope you and your loved one will.

A New Perspective on the Process of Change

Behavior changes with behavior changes. The process of change can be complicated and uneven, and it takes time. Patterns of substance use and other compulsive behaviors tend to be incredibly complex, with many biopsychosocial factors contributing to creating and maintaining habits; finding the right set of strategies and support to help new habits take hold will not happen in a flash.

Change is a process of mastery, which takes time, patience, compassion, and practice.

An important part of mastery is that over time, and with practice, the different ideas and skills you're learning start to operate together in a connected way. And that is a big deal. Beginning piano players only see the notes one at a time; pianists see whole chords and phrases, melody and harmony, notes and rests, and how they relate to each other to make music. You'll find that with practice, the different parts of ITC start to combine in ways that make sense become even more powerful.

What does this look like? Things like realizing you feel good about reinforcing their early night in with a hug (Helping with Action—Behavior Reinforcement) because you truly understand how hard it was for them to make the decision to come home (Helping with Understanding— Behaviors Make Sense), and you're aware of how this hug you gave them supports your core values of connection and respect (Helping with Awareness—Self-Awareness), while also being aware of how vulnerable you feel in opening your heart to them again after yesterday's fight (Helping with Awareness—Willingness).

With practice, you'll increasingly get a feeling for how the parts of ITC fit together and reinforce each other. You may also realize over time that this approach is helpful throughout your life, not just for helping someone with changes around substance use. In other words, this is about your creating the life you want with all the people you care about, one that is grounded in kindness, respect, collaboration, and support for positive activities and your core values.

We'll say it again: change comes by addition, not subtraction. There is no delete-all or "unlearn" button that can erase old behaviors. Can you imagine unlearning to ride a bicycle? Change is the process of learning new behaviors that can replace the old, but the memory and connection to the old behaviors don't disappear.

For a fun way to start to understand this, you can try the following exercise.

Holding a pen or pencil in your *nondominant* hand, write the sentence below three times (remember, with your nondominant hand!):

Practice is the effort that makes things possible.

____

____

____

How did it feel to write with your nondominant hand? What thoughts did you have as you were writing? What did you have to do differently to write this way? You could probably feel how hard the task was to complete. And you can probably see how, with some practice, you could get better at writing with your nondominant hand than you currently can.

The process of learning new behaviors, for both you and your loved one, may be similarly unintuitive at first. When we start to learn a new skill, we typically feel awkward and may even avoid trying because it seems too difficult. Our minds chime in with criticism and impatience. Any new behavior requires practice to become easier and more automatic; eventually, you gain confidence, and it requires less mental energy to perform the behavior—whether the behavior in question is learning to play the piano, learning to replace substance use with something else, or learning to respond differently.

Why Practice, Practice, (and Even More) Practice Matters

Seeing change as a learning process that requires practice helps in many ways. First, it can help increase your empathy and patience for your loved one as they go through the inevitable ups and downs along this journey. Second, it can help you remember that old behaviors don't disappear with the snap of a finger; your loved one first has to manage the uncomfortable thoughts and feelings that come with trying to learn a new skill. Next, understanding this learning process can help you respond in ways that are consistent with the person you want to be. Finally, it can make it easier to have compassion for your own attempts at new ways of helping, which may be far from perfect at times.

Over time, getting past the awkwardness of "practice" will not only give you a sense of ease, but also allow you to take the ITC approach with greater skill and effectiveness. Thus, your helping to create the conditions for change will also be reinforcing for you! As you see how helpful and effective all this is, you'll be rewarded—not with instant change, but with a sense of helpfulness, purpose, greater connection, and ultimately, hope.

You Can't Get It Right Every Time

As you practice with ITC tools and strategies, you might get frustrated and be tempted to give up. You might say to yourself, *This isn't working*, *This isn't me*, or *I can't do this*. Such thoughts and impulses are normal when you're learning; they are part of the process, not a reason to quit. What's more, if you give up after one or two failed attempts, little will change. But if you keep trying, learn from your missteps, and use that information to plan your next effort, the new behavior will strengthen over time and improvements will come. Also, remember self-compassion. We're all human, and being hard on ourselves or expecting perfection won't get us the results we want any more than giving up will.

Practice again and again. You can use the exercises in this book and others (like journaling) to track your efforts to create a record you can look back on, to help you remember what you're doing, when you're doing it, and how it's actually going—which might differ from how it feels like it's going on a bad day. If you've done all the exercises in this book, you can check out our additional online resources (see page 197). As you go, we recommend saving them to look back on. By tracking, you can draw connections between your efforts and their effect on the well-being of your loved one, your family, and yourself.

Consider the following testimony from a parent using ITC for an example of what the work, in progress, might look like.

> *I've been practicing these strategies for four months. Overall, I see improvement in my daughter. I'm not where I want to be, and neither is she, but I see progress. But I honestly have to do a lot of self-talk to stop myself from going back to old patterns, like yelling at*

her when she uses. I must constantly remind myself that yelling does not stop her from using. And while things are not perfect, there are not only significant reductions in her use, but a new emergence of self-awareness and insight. I almost cried when she told me that drinking and smoking do not make her happy! Most importantly, I feel better about myself and do not experience the internal conflict that raged within me before starting this approach.

Parting Words

We hope you feel ready—and inspired—to take the tools and ideas in this guide and practice using them in your own life. We hope you see how they can help improve your well-being and the well-being of your loved one and your entire family. Now, we want to leave you with these thoughts:

1. **Thank you.** For caring. For being an advocate for your loved one. For learning to be an advocate for yourself. For allowing yourself to be human and to feel all the feelings that come with the struggle—confusion, anger, fear, and hopelessness, but also love, compassion, and hope. Thank you.

2. **You can make a difference!** It's understandable to feel stuck and overwhelmed on occasion. You may dwell on the things you wish you'd done differently in the past. You may feel tired. At times you may think nothing will ever change. When you're scared and feeling mistreated, positive reinforcement doesn't come easily. We appreciate your trying in spite of all this. We know you can have a positive impact on your loved one—and on almost every area of your life—and hope you'll have compassion for yourself along the way.

3. **Taking an active role in helping your loved one does not make you "codependent" or "an enabler."** The issue is not whether staying connected and involved makes your loved one more likely to use, but whether you're being strategic as to which behaviors you reinforce (remember Ray and his garden).

4. **Change can be hard, but you don't have to get it perfect to have a positive impact, and you get to keep trying.** Practice, practice, practice. Being aware of your thoughts and feelings and basing your actions on your values offer you a better

shot at being patient with yourself and your loved one. You've likely tried to help them change many times. Isn't it worth trying something different?

5. **Change does not usually happen overnight.** You might feel discouraged if your efforts to positively reinforce healthy behaviors don't result in changes right away. Let yourself take baby steps. Use your ITC tools (they're your tools now!) to make small improvements to your own self-care so that you have more resources and feel less distressed. You'll then be better equipped to increase and further improve the positive interactions between you and your loved one. Small improvements build confidence and create the foundation for substantive, long-lasting change for everyone involved.

6. **Kindness matters.** The saying "You catch more flies with honey than vinegar" has been proven by research. It's more effective to help someone consider change with kind words than with criticism (Apodaca et al. 2016). We hope that this has become clearer and clearer with each chapter of this guide, but it bears repeating: kindness matters. A lot. For you, for your loved one, for everyone. It's not always the easiest route, but it almost always helps. Science + Kindness = Change.

7. **You are not alone.** An invitation to change doesn't happen alone. At a minimum, it takes two people, but as you've gathered by now, hopefully, it's bigger than that. The ITC wheel expands with use, embracing you and your loved one, your family, your friends, and other people you reach out to with these tools and ideas, and on out from your home to your local community to the broader ITC community of people trying to see and do things in new, more helpful ways.

Best of luck to you and your loved one as you begin the process of change.

Would you like to start an Invitation to Change group in your community? CMC: Foundation for Change is committed to supporting grassroots access to evidence-based ideas and practices, and we wholeheartedly encourage readers to support each other through the Invitation to Change process. For more resources to help you use this guide in a group setting, please visit our website at http://www.cmcffc.org/resources.

Acknowledgements

First and foremost, we'd like to thank all the parents and family members who helped us write this workbook. Everything we know about motivation and change comes from our experiences of sharing the best that science has to offer with you and witnessing how you apply it to your lives. The concepts in this book were honed through years of working with family members whose pain, wisdom, and personal experiences shaped what we hope is a powerful resource for anyone who wants to help (friends, treatment professionals, first responders, faith-based leaders, educators, etc.). Thank you to all the families with whom we have worked over the years—our hearts have hurt for you and have been blessed by sharing in your journey. You are the reason we developed ITC. It is yours to use and to share.

We are ever grateful for the work of our CMC:FFC team: Meg Murray, Elliot Foote, Andre Sim, Amy Milin, Kayla Brady, and Tianna Soto. Your respect for our mission and the fact that you each spend all day, every day, trying to help bring compassion to families that so desperately need it is never taken for granted.

We are honored to work with our trainers who bring the Invitation to Change to life for families and professionals around the country: Cordelia Kraus, Nicole Kosanke, Cindy Brody, Brooke Monaco, Josh King, Rachel Proujansky, Tanya Beecher, Cathy Tellides, Jarell Myers, Lori Siegal, Julie Jarvis, Pam Jones, Emily Cavell, Dana Gruber, and Jonathan Fader.

We want to say a very special thank you to the professionals and family members who donated their time to edit this text and ensure it spoke to diverse communities: Henry Zhu, Jaime Cooper, Paul Kusiak, Cordelia Kraus, Jarell Myers, Nicole Kosanke, Catherine Hogan, and Tom Hedrick.

We also thank the generous donors who fund CMC:FFC. We are fully supported by your generosity and ITC would not exist without it. You are helping create a resource for everyone hoping to help someone struggling with substance use and we thank you.

We offer a shout out of deep appreciation to the visionaries in our field of helping: Bob Meyers, Jane Smith, Bill Miller, Alan Marlatt, Kelly Wilson, Steven Hayes, Richard Ryan, Kristen Neff, and Chris Germer. You put the evidence in "evidence-based" and we honor all the effort and commitment we know that entails.

We are forever thankful to Stephanie Higgs, who sprinkles her language magic ("Stephanizing") over our writing. Our books would not be jargon-free without you.

And finally, to our families—we could not do this without your loving support. We know that our hours trying to help others pulls us away from you. We hope that you know that time (your time) is hopefully making the world a better place and that you take pride in this work. It is yours as well.

In memoriam, we thank Tom Hedrick, whose huge heart helped us find our way to creating ITC. His love for every parent trying to help a child with substance problems is why we exist.

Resources

For downloadable copies of the exercises in this book, some bonus ones that might be helpful to you, and a copy of the glossary, visit the publisher's website at http://www.newharbinger.com/50188.

For even more resources, including our family and friends newsletter, information on special topics such as trauma, a group guide, and new exercises and other materials that we're developing all the time, visit http://www.cmcffc.org.

For information about our services and treatment options for family members, friends, and individuals struggling with substance use, go to http://www.motivationandchange.com.

For More Information

About drug effects
http://www.drugabuse.gov/drug-topics

Addiction and the Family: International Network
http://www.afinetwork.info

National Institute on Alcoholism and Alcohol Abuse (NIAAA)
http://www.niaaa.nih.gov

National Institute on Drug Abuse (NIDA)
http://www.drugabuse.gov

Robert J. Meyers and CRAFT
http://www.robertjmeyersphd.com/craft.html

Substance Abuse and Mental Health Services Administration (SAMHSA)
http://www.samhsa.gov

For Help and Support

Al-Anon (support groups)
http://www.al-anon.org

Allies in Recovery
http://www.alliesinrecovery.net

American Academy of Addiction Psychiatry (find a psychiatrist)
http://www.aaap.org/education/resources/patients

Association for Behavioral and Cognitive Therapies
http://www.abct.org/get-help

Behavioral Tech (Dialectical Behavior Therapy)
http://www.behavioraltech.org/resources/find-a-therapist

Checkup and Choices
http://www.checkupandchoices.com/drinkers-checkup

Faces and Voices of Recovery (advocacy and information)
http://www.facesandvoicesofrecovery.org

Families for Addiction Support (Canada)
http://www.farcanada.org

Nar-Anon (support groups)
http://www.nar-anon.org

OneLife Education & Training (for professionals)
http://www.onelifellc.com

Partnership to End Addiction
http://www.drugfree.org

SAMHSA Treatment Locator
http://www.samhsa.gov/find-help/treatment

SMART Recovery (support groups)
http://www.smartrecovery.org/family

Sober Families
http://www.soberfamilies.com

THRIVE! Family Support
http://www.thrivefamilysupport.org

Further Reading

Beyond Addiction: How Science and Kindness Help People Change. Jeffrey Foote, PhD, Carrie Wilkens, PhD, and Nicole Kosanke, PhD, with Stephanie Higgs.

Beautiful Boy: A Father's Journey Through His Son's Addiction. David Sheff.

Full Catastrophe Living: Using the Wisdom of Your Body and Mind to Face Stress, Pain, and Illness. Jon Kabat-Zinn, PhD.

Get Out of Your Mind and Into Your Life: The New Acceptance and Commitment Therapy. Steven C. Hayes, PhD, with Spencer Smith.

Get Your Loved One Sober: Alternatives to Nagging, Pleading, and Threatening. Robert J. Meyers, PhD, and Brenda L. Wolfe, PhD.

Inside Rehab: The Surprising Truth About Addiction Treatment and How to Get Help That Works and *Sober for Good: New Solutions for Drinking Problems—Advice from Those Who Have Succeeded*. Anne Fletcher.

The Joy of Parenting: An Acceptance and Commitment Therapy Guide to Effective Parenting in the Early Years. Lisa Coyne and Amy R. Murrel.

Lighthouse Conversations: Being a Beacon for Teens. Jennifer Ollis Blomqvist.

Listening Well: The Art of Empathic Understanding. William R. Miller, PhD.

The Mindful Self-Compassion Workbook: A Proven Way to Accept Yourself, Build Inner Strength, and Thrive. Kristin Neff, PhD, and Christopher Germer, PhD.

On Second Thought: How Ambivalence Shapes Your Life. William R. Miller.

Over the Influence: The Harm Reduction Guide to Controlling Your Drug and Alcohol Use. 2nd Ed. Pat Denning and Jeannie Little.

Self-Compassion: The Proven Power of Being Kind to Yourself. Kristin Neff, PhD.

Unbroken Brain: A Revolutionary New Way of Understanding Addiction. Maia Szalavitz.

Wisdom to Know the Difference: An Acceptance and Commitment Therapy Workbook for Overcoming Substance Abuse. Kelly G. Wilson.

Emergency Resources

9-1-1

Domestic violence hotline (US): 1-800-799-7233

Poison control hotline (US): 1-800-222-1222

Suicide hotline (US): 1-800-273-8255

Glossary

affirmations: Comments that explicitly acknowledge the positive. Unlike general cheerleading, affirmations applaud specific actions or situations.

ambivalence: The feeling of wanting two opposing or conflicting things at the same time.

aversive strategies: Strategies that attempt to control or stop another person's behavior. Examples include shouting, screaming, lecturing, or inflicting emotional or physical pain; also criticizing, shaming, or labeling. Proven to be ineffective.

behavior analysis (also functional analysis): Analyzing the people, circumstances, and experiences associated with a behavior such as substance use to understand what is reinforcing it—which reasonable, basic human need(s) the behavior meets.

biopsychosocial: A single term referring to the multiple factors that influence people's behavior: biology, psychology, and social contexts.

conversational red light: Any of several kinds of signals including body language, tone of voice, and words like "not now" that people in conversation give each other to warn that they don't want to go where the conversation is headed.

conversational trap: Automatic, often emotional responses to not feeling like you're heard or on the same team. Examples include lecturing, blaming, and taking sides, and they tend to push communication into a worse place rather than a better one.

information sandwich: A three-step communication technique for making the information that you want to share (the contents of the "sandwich") palatable to someone: first, ask permission; second, provide the information; third, check back.

ITC: The acronym for the Invitation to Change approach, focusing on inviting rather than forcing someone to change through understanding, awareness, and action; what this book is all about.

LOVE: The acronym for a communication strategy based on Listening, Offering information, Validating, and Empathizing.

motivational hooks: Reasons for seeking help that are most meaningful to the person you're speaking to about getting help.

natural consequences: The unwanted costs that organically happen as a result of a behavior, when no one interferes; the opposite of positive reinforcement.

OARS: The acronym for a skillful listening strategy based on asking Open-ended questions, Affirming, Reflecting back, and Summarizing.

open-ended questions: Questions that begin with words or phrases such as "how," "what," or "please tell me more about"—and can't be answered with one word, such as "yes" or "no." They invite description and set a collaborative tone, as they communicate interest in the other person's view.

positive reinforcement: Responding to a behavior you'd like to see more of in a way that makes it more likely to happen again.

present moment awareness: Awareness of your own internal experiences as they happen.

reflections (also called active listening): Restating some or all of what you think someone has said. Reflections communicate to the other person that you're listening and trying to understand what they're saying.

reinforcer: An outcome of a behavior that makes it more likely that the behavior will be repeated. Generally, an increase in something desirable like pleasure or human connection, or a decrease in something undesirable like boredom or physical pain.

self compassion: mindfulness (what we call self-awareness), as opposed to getting stuck in your feelings and thoughts; self-kindness, as opposed to self-judgment; and common humanity, as opposed to isolation (Neff 2003).

simply listening: Paying attention to what another person is saying and trying to understand them. Can involve gestures like making eye contact or nodding your head, but requires that you do not interrupt, talk over, or comment in a way that stops the other person from talking.

skillful listening: Builds on simply listening with considerate, empathetic responding. A mnemonic for four skillful listening tools is the acronym OARS: Asking open-ended questions, Affirming, Reflecting back, and Summarizing.

SURF: The acronym for a communication strategy that calls for being Specific, offering an Understanding statement, taking partial Responsibility, and labeling your Feelings.

willingness: Being willing to allow for the vulnerability and pain that come with caring.

References

Amrhein, P. C., W. R. Miller, C. E. Yahne, M. Palmer, and L. Fulcher. 2003. "Client Commitment Language During Motivational Interviewing Predicts Drug Use Outcomes." *Journal of Consulting and Clinical Psychology* 71(5): 862–878.

Apodaca, T. R., K. M. Jackson, B. Borsari, M. Magill, R. Longabaugh, N. R. Mastroleo, and N. P. Barnett. 2016. "Which Individual Therapist Behaviors Elicit Client Change Talk and Sustain Talk in Motivational Interviewing?" *Journal of Substance Abuse Treatment* 61: 60–65.

Ariss, T., and C. E. Fairbairn. 2020. "The Effect of Significant Other Involvement in Treatment for Substance Use Disorders: A Meta-Analysis." *Journal of Consulting and Clinical Psychology* 88(6): 526–540.

Azrin, N. H. 1976. "Improvements in the Community Reinforcement Approach to Alcoholism." *Behavior Research and Therapy* 14: 339–348.

Bien, T. H., W. R. Miller, and J. S. Tonigan. 1993. "Brief Interventions for Alcohol Problems: A Review." *Addiction* 88(3): 315–336.

Brigham, G. S., N. Slesnicke, T. M. Winhusen, D. F. Lewis, X. Guo, and E. Somoza. 2014. "A Randomized Pilot Clinical Trial to Evaluate the Efficacy of Community Reinforcement and Family Training for Treatment Retention (CRAFT-T) for Improving Outcomes for Patients Completing Opioid Detoxification." *Drug and Alcohol Dependence* 138: 240–243.

Downey, L., D. B. Rosengren, and D. Donovan. 2001. "Sources of Motivation for Abstinence: A Replication Analysis of the Reasons for Quitting Questionnaire." *Addictive Behaviors* 26(1): 79–89.

Foote, J., C. Wilkens, and N. Kosanke, with Stephanie Higgs. 2014. *Beyond Addiction: How Science and Kindness Help People Change.* New York: Scribner.

Ginley, M. K., R. A. Pfund, C. J. Rash, and K. Zajac. 2021. "Long-Term Efficacy of Contingency Management Based on Objective Indicators of Abstinence from Illicit Substance Use Up to 1 Year Following Treatment: A Meta-Analysis." *Journal of Consulting and Clinical Psychology* 89(1): 58–71.

Grant, B. F., R. Goldstein, T. D. Saha, P. Chou, J. Jung, H. Zhang, R. P. Pickering, W. J. Ruan, S. M. Smith, B. Huang, and D. S. Hasin. 2015. "Epidemiology of DSM-5 Alcohol Use Disorder: Results from the National Epidemiologic Survey on Alcohol and Related Conditions III." *JAMA Psychiatry* 72(8): 757–766.

Hadland, S. E., T. W. Park, and S. M. Bagley. 2018. "Stigma Associated with Medication Treatment for Young Adults with Opioid Use Disorder: A Case Series." *Addiction, Science and Clinical Practice* 13.

Hasin, D. S., C. P. O'Brien, M. Auriacombe, G. Borges, K. Bucholz, A. Budney, W. M. Compton, et al. 2013. "DSM-5 Criteria for Substance Use Disorders: Recommendations and Rationale." *The American Journal of Psychiatry* 170(8): 834–851.

Hayes, S. C., K. Strosahl, and K. G. Wilson. 2012. *Acceptance and Commitment Therapy: The Process and Practice of Mindful Change*. New York: Guilford Press.

Higgins, S. T., S. H. Heil, and J. P. Lussier. 2004. "Clinical Implications of Reinforcement as a Determinant of Substance Use Disorders." *Annual Review of Psychology* 55: 431–461.

Iguchi, M. Y., M. A. Belding, A. R. Morral, and R. J. Lamb. 1997. "Reinforcing Operants Other Than Abstinence in Drug Abuse Treatment: An Effective Alternative for Reducing Drug Use." *Journal of Consulting and Clinical Psychology* 65(3): 421–428.

Marlatt, G., J. S. Baer, D. M. Donovan, and D. R. Kivlahan. 1988. "Addictive Behaviors: Etiology and Treatment." *Annual Review of Psychology* 39: 223–252.

Marlowe, D. B., E. P. Merikle, K. C. Kirby, D. S. Festinger, and A. T. McLellan. 2001. "Multidimensional Assessment of Perceived Treatment-Entry Pressures Among Substance Abusers." *Psychology of Addictive Behaviors* 15(2): 97–108.

Meyers, R. J., W. R. Miller, D. E. Hill, and J. S. Tonigan. 1999. "Community Reinforcement and Family Training (CRAFT): Engaging Unmotivated Drug Users in Treatment." *Journal of Substance Abuse* 10(3): 291–308.

Meyers, R. J., M. Villanueva, and J. E. Smith. 2005. "The Community Reinforcement Approach: History and New Directions." *Journal of Cognitive Psychotherapy: An International Quarterly* 19(3): 247–60.

Miller, W. R. 1985. "Motivation for Treatment: A Review with Special Emphasis on Alcoholism." *Psychological Bulletin* 98(1): 84–107.

Miller, W. R., R. G. Benefield, and S. T. Tonigan. 1993. "Enhancing Motivation for Change in Problem Drinking: A Controlled Comparison of Two Therapist Styles." *Journal of Consulting and Clinical Psychology* 61(3): 455–461.

Miller, W. R., A. A. Forcehimes, and A. Zweben. 2019. *Treating Addiction: A Guide for Professionals*. 2nd ed. New York: Guilford Press.

Miller, W. R., R. J. Meyers, and J. S. Tonigan. 1999. "Engaging the Unmotivated in Treatment for Alcohol Problems: A Comparison of Three Strategies for Intervention Through Family Members." *Journal of Consulting and Clinical Psychology* 67(5): 688–697.

Miller, W. R., and S. Rollnick. 2013. *Motivational Interviewing: Helping People Change*. 3rd ed. New York: Guilford Press.

Moyers, T. B., and T. Martin. 2006. "Therapist Influence on Client Language During Motivational Interviewing Sessions." *Journal of Substance Abuse Treatment* 30(3): 245–251.

Moyers, T. B., T. Martin, P. J. Christopher, J. M. Houck, J. S. Tonigan, and P. C. Amrhein. 2007. "Client Language as a Mediator of Motivational Interviewing Efficacy: Where Is the Evidence?" *Alcoholism: Clinical and Experimental Research* 31(10 Suppl): 40s–47s.

National Institute on Drug Abuse (NIDA). 2020. "Evidence-Based Approaches to Drug Addiction Treatment." *Principles of Drug Addiction Treatment: A Research-Based Guide*. 3rd ed. Accessed December 6, 2021. https://www.drugabuse.gov/publications/principles-drug-addiction-treatment-research-based-guide-third-edition/evidence-based-approaches-to-drug-addiction-treatment.

Neff, K. D. 2003. "Self-Compassion: An Alternative Conceptualization of a Healthy Attitude Toward Oneself." *Self and Identity* 2: 85–101.

Neff, K. D., and D. J. Faso. 2014. "Self-Compassion and Well-Being in Parents of Children with Autism." *Mindfulness* 6(4): 938–947.

Neff, K. D., K. Kirkpatrick, and S. S. Rude. 2007. "Self-Compassion and Adaptive Psychological Functioning." *Journal of Research in Personality* 41: 139–154.

Ozbay, F., D. C. Johnson, E. Dimoulas, C. A. Morgan III, D. Charney, and S. Southwick. 2007. "Social Support and Resilience to Stress: From Neurobiology to Clinical Practice." *Psychiatry* 4(5): 35–40.

Petry, N. M. 2012. *Contingency Management for Substance Abuse Treatment: A Guide to Implementing This Evidence-Based Practice*. New York: Routledge.

Reblin, M., and B. N. Uchino. 2008. "Social and Emotional Support and Its Implication for Health." *Current Opinion in Psychiatry* 21(2): 201–205.

Robertson, E. B., S. L. David, and S. A. Rao. 2003. *Preventing Drug Use Among Children and Adolescents: A Research-Based Guide for Parents, Educators, and Community Leaders*. 2nd ed. NIH Publication No. 04-4212(A). Bethesda, MD: National Institute on Drug Abuse.

Smedslund, G., R. C. Berg, K. T. Hammerstrøm, A. Steiro, K. A. Leikness, H. M. Dahl, and K. Karlsen. 2011. "Motivational Interviewing for Substance Abuse." *Cochrane Database of Systematic Reviews* 5: CD008063.

Substance Abuse and Mental Health Services Administration (SAMHSA). 2019. *TIP 35: Enhancing Motivation for Change in Substance Use Disorder Treatment*. DHHS Publication No. PEP19-02-01-003. Rockville, MD: Substance Abuse and Mental Health Services Administration. Accessed December 6, 2021. https://store.samhsa.gov/product/TIP-35-Enhancing-Motivation-for-Change-in-Substance-Use-Disorder-Treatment/PEP19-02-01-003.

Uhl, G. R., G. F. Koob, and J. Cable. 2019. "The Neurobiology of Addiction." *Annals of the New York Academy of Sciences* 1451(1): 5–28.

White, W. L., and W. R. Miller. 2007. "The Use of Confrontation in Addiction Treatment: History, Science, and Time for Change." *Counselor* 8(4): 12–30.

Wilson, K. 2017. "A Meditation with Kelly Wilson for Overcoming Substance Abuse." Filmed January 27, 2017. Webinar, *ACT for Overcoming Substance Abuse*. Accessed December 6, 2021. https://www.praxiscet.com/posts/mediation-overcoming-substance-abuse.

Yang, L., L. Y. Wong, M. M. Grivel, and D. Hasin. 2017. "Stigma and Substance Use Disorders: An International Phenomenon." *Current Opinion in Psychiatry* 30(5): 378–388.

Jeffrey Foote, PhD, is cofounder of the Center for Motivation and Change (CMC) outpatient programs in New York City, NY; Long Island, NY; and Washington, DC; and residential program CMC: Berkshires in Western Massachusetts. He is also cofounder and executive director of the CMC: Foundation for Change, a nonprofit organization with the mission of improving the dissemination of evidence-based ideas and strategies to the families of persons struggling with substance use. Additionally, he is coauthor of the award-winning book, *Beyond Addiction*—a practical guide for families dealing with addiction and substance problems in a loved one, based on principles of Community Reinforcement and Family Training (CRAFT). Foote is also a contributor to two workbooks combining strategies from CRAFT: *The Parent's 20 Minute Guide* and *The Partner's 20 Minute Guide,* which offer specific tools and practice in evidence-based strategies for helping a loved one change.

Kenneth Carpenter, PhD, is director of training for the CMC and CMC: Foundation for Change. He is a licensed clinical psychologist and research scientist, and has held academic and research scientist positions at New York-based universities and state agencies. Carpenter has received federal and private foundation grant money for investigating the psychological, behavioral, and neurobiological factors associated with substance use, and developing evidence-based motivational and cognitive behavioral strategies for helping individuals make important lifestyle changes.

Carrie Wilkens, PhD, is cofounder and clinical director of the CMC in New York City, NY; Long Island, NY; and Washington, DC. She is cofounder of CMC: Berkshires, a private inpatient/residential program employing the same treatment approaches in Western Massachusetts. She is also cofounder and president of the CMC: Foundation for Change, a nonprofit organization with the mission of improving the dissemination of evidence-based ideas and strategies to professionals and loved ones of persons struggling with substance use through the Invitation to Change approach. Wilkens coauthored the award-winning book, *Beyond Addiction* with Jeff Foote, and coauthored a user-friendly workbook for parents, *The Parent's 20 Minute Guide.*

ABOUT US

Founded by psychologist Matthew McKay and Patrick Fanning, New Harbinger has published books that promote wellness in mind, body, and spirit for more than forty-five years.

Our proven-effective self-help books and pioneering workbooks help readers of all ages and backgrounds make positive lifestyle changes, improve mental health and well-being, and achieve meaningful personal growth. In addition, our spirituality books offer profound guidance for deepening awareness and cultivating healing, self-discovery, and fulfillment.

New Harbinger is proud to be an independent and employee-owned company, publishing books that reflect its core values of integrity, innovation, commitment, sustainability, compassion, and trust. Written by leaders in the field and recommended by therapists worldwide, New Harbinger books are practical, reliable, and provide real tools for real change.

MORE BOOKS from NEW HARBINGER PUBLICATIONS

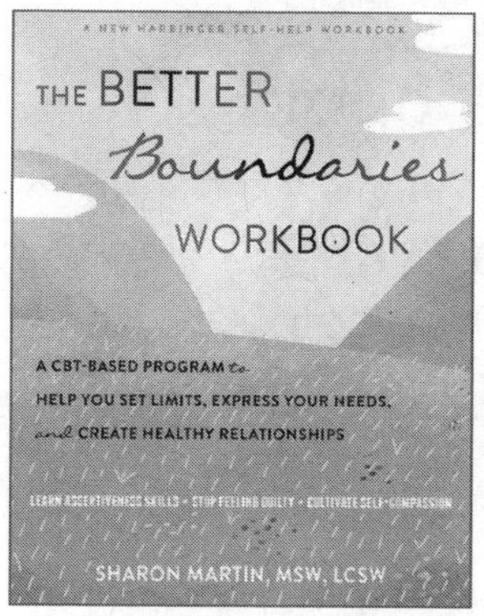

THE BETTER BOUNDARIES WORKBOOK

A CBT-Based Program to Help You Set Limits, Express Your Needs, and Create Healthy Relationships

978-1684037582 / US $24.95

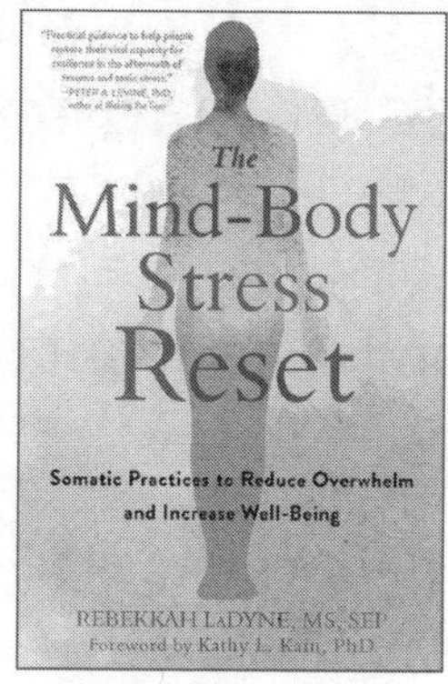

THE MIND-BODY STRESS RESET

Somatic Practices to Reduce Overwhelm and Increase Well-Being

978-1684034277 / US $17.95

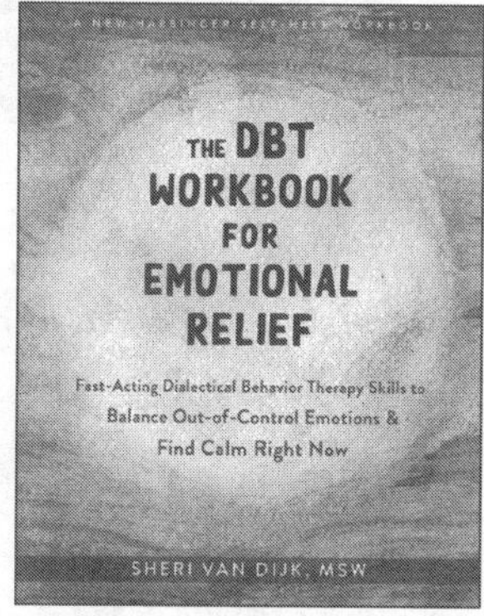

THE DBT WORKBOOK FOR EMOTIONAL RELIEF

Fast-Acting Dialectical Behavior Therapy Skills to Balance Out-of-Control Emotions and Find Calm Right Now

978-1684039647 / US $24.95

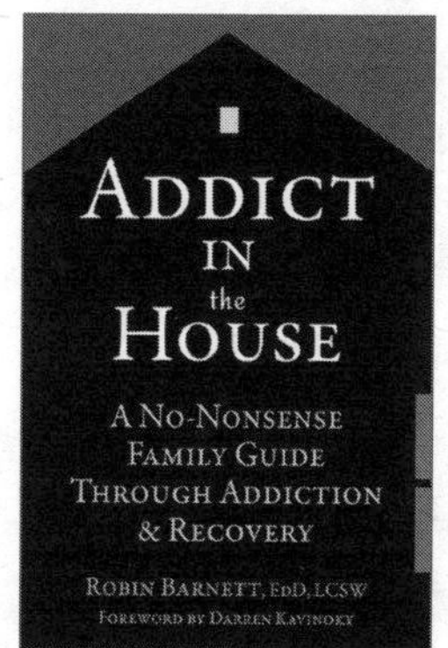

ADDICT IN THE HOUSE

A No-Nonsense Family Guide Through Addiction and Recovery

978-1626252608 / US $16.95

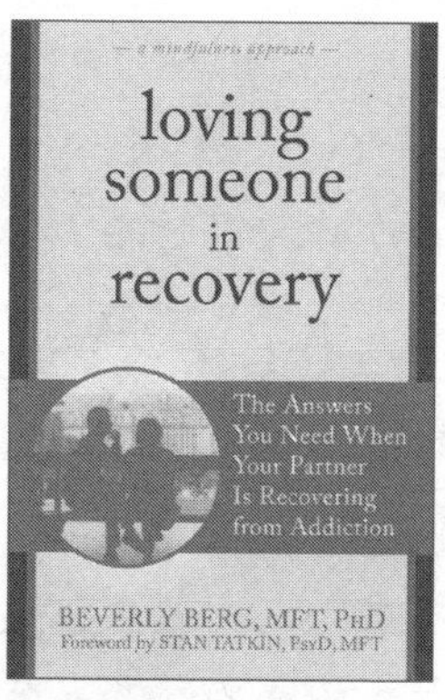

LOVING SOMEONE IN RECOVERY

The Answers You Need When Your Partner Is Recovering from Addiction

978-1608828982 / US $21.95

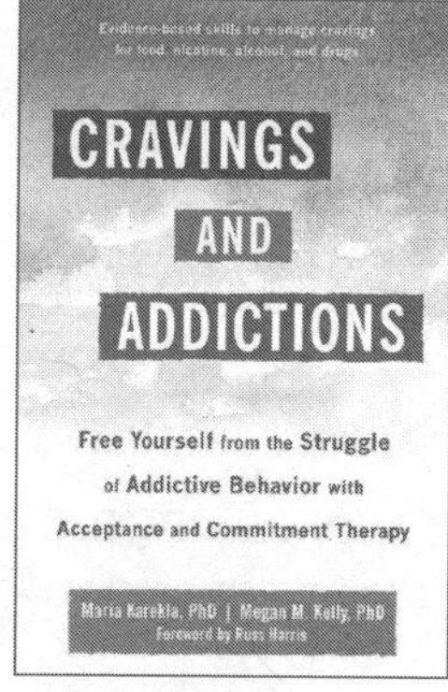

CRAVINGS AND ADDICTIONS

Free Yourself from the Struggle of Addictive Behavior with Acceptance and Commitment Therapy

978-1684038336 / US $17.95

new**harbinger**publications

1-800-748-6273 / newharbinger.com

(VISA, MC, AMEX / prices subject to change without notice)

Follow Us

Don't miss out on new books from New Harbinger.
Subscribe to our email list at **newharbinger.com/subscribe**

Did you know there are **free tools** you can download for this book?

Free tools are things like **worksheets**, **guided meditation exercises**, and **more** that will help you get the most out of your book.

You can download free tools for this book—whether you bought or borrowed it, in any format, from any source—from the New Harbinger website. All you need is a NewHarbinger.com account. Just use the URL provided in this book to view the free tools that are available for it. Then, click on the "download" button for the free tool you want, and follow the prompts that appear to log in to your NewHarbinger.com account and download the material.

You can also save the free tools for this book to your **Free Tools Library** so you can access them again anytime, just by logging in to your account! Just look for this button on the book's free tools page.

+ Save this to my free tools library

If you need help accessing or downloading free tools, visit **newharbinger.com/faq** or contact us at **customerservice@newharbinger.com.**